NOT MY

Stuff

God loves you and is counting on you to manage His stuff wisely.
The first step is to look at everything and say:
It's Not My Stuff!

NOT MY
Stuff

Ed Holland

ISBN: 978-1-947153-44-8

Cover Design   Eowyn Riggins

Interior Layout   Rachel Newhouse

To Kathy, my best friend and lifelong partner

This book is only possible because together we have lived out the principles found in its pages. Over the years you have been a fulltime muse, sometimes a ghost whispering in my ear, and especially an honest and essential editor.
Thank you for all you do and for choosing me, I love you.

Ed

DEDICATION

If you have an open heart, there will be moments in your life when you recognize that God has put someone special in your path. What at first appears to be a random meeting, is really a divine appointment. I was favored with such a moment in the summer of 2007 when I met Bob and Julie Myers.

Bob was small in stature and my first impression was that he was somewhat unassuming, meek, and even a little shy. Little did I know, there was a giant man of faith within that modest shell of clay.

Bob and I saw the world very much alike, and as Bob would often say, the smartest people are always the ones who see the world as you see it. Our similarities did not stop Bob from challenging me when my thinking was fuzzy or lacked logic.

Our first meeting turned into a regular event. We laughed together; we transparently shared our burdens. We talked about family and politics, but our discussions always ended up on the same subject. We talked about ways Jesus's Church could effectively impact more lives.

Together with his wife Julie, Bob had built a business from the ground up. His insights into the local community's business trends, and what the future would bring, always helped me as I attempted to make wise decisions as a church leader.

Over the next decade of time that I would know Bob, I would not make a major decision without first asking him for his input. I'm sure he saved me from myself on several occasions. He was not only gracious with his time and thoughts, but he was a generous giver as he and Julie faithfully supported several ministries in our community.

Bob loved giving to projects that changed lives and met needs. So, when our church needed to replace hundreds of windows in our aging facilities, he stepped up and started writing checks. To him the math was simple. Energy efficient windows equaled reduced utility bills; reduced bills equaled more money for life-changing ministry.

Then came the day I met with Bob to ask his advice about a possible relocation and rebirth of our church. I was filled with angst. Since Bob had invested nearly a quarter of a million dollars to replace the windows of that aging building, I was naturally concerned about how he would feel about leaving that investment behind. Bob listened to the vision I had for the future attentively and then, without hesitation, he said, "This move sounds like the wise thing to do. The money

I gave was not my money when I gave it. Everything I have belongs to God. It's not my stuff."

Bob, I know you are in heaven right now, but I still want to thank you for teaching us with your life that the things of this world do not belong to us. I will never forget the day you said, "None of it belongs to me, it's NOT MY STUFF."

CONTENTS

Stuff – It's all around us

Not long ago my wife Kathy asked me to go to the antique mall with her. This is something she used to do with her dad. They would go antiquing for hours, which meant that I didn't have to. But since her dad passed away I had apparently been nominated to take his place. (I don't remember accepting the position.) Usually, I have an excuse ready, which involves just about anything other than antiquing. For some reason that day her question caught me off guard, so I didn't have a handy excuse ready. I think I panicked, and I must have agreed to go because shortly thereafter I found myself smack dab in the middle of yesteryear!

I'm amazed that Kathy can walk around in this huge, old, unairconditioned building and look at a bunch of old stuff that seemingly no one wants anymore. Occasionally, she would pick up a rusty kitchen utensil and say, "Oh look, my mom had one of these." Or "I remember using one of these when I was a little girl." I want to say, "So?" But I stay calm, pretend to be interested and say "Oh." We move on for what seems like hours but looking at my watch I realize that time moves very slowly in an antique mall.

I know my wife enjoys things like this, and because I love her, I can "do the time." But in all reality, I just don't get it. Old long play albums, posters of dead cowboys, grandma's old dresses, porcelain dolls, and one-eyed teddy bears that would frighten most children. All I see is a bunch of relics (dare I say junk?) that used to be important, but now have no use, no purpose, and no value beyond the memory of something that once was. And while those memories are important, it still makes me think about what the Bible said, *For what is your life? It is even a vapor that appears for a little time and then vanishes away* (James 4:14, NKJV). And if our very lives are vanishing vapors, then what about all the stuff that we've accumulated during our life? And really that's all it is – stuff. Temporary. Here today and gone tomorrow. Must haves. Shiny objects. Things that fade away. And yet, everywhere you look, stuff is all around us.

Perhaps you've seen the Expedia commercial with Ewan McGregor trying to convince us we should travel more. He says, "Stuff, we love stuff." He rattles off a list of amazing stuff out there that we can buy and then says, "I doubt many of us will look back on our lives and think, I wish I would have gotten a sportier SUV, or even a thinner TV, or found a trendier scent. But the commercial ends with McGregor's final question, "Do you think any of us will look back on our life and regret the things we didn't buy?" The commercial struck a chord with me because I agree – people just can't seem to get enough stuff!

Then later I came across an article about the self-storage industry that caught my attention. Did you know that in the United States alone, the self-storage industry has an annual revenue of over 39 billion dollars? There are presently over 49,000 self-storage units across this great land of ours, with 1.9 billion square feet of rentable space. It is also estimated that over 10 percent of the population pays an average of 89 dollars a month to store their stuff.[1]

Why?

Are our houses really so small? Do we not have closets or garages for all our stuff? Or could it be that we just have too much stuff to begin with? Think about all those Amazon boxes on the front porch each week, or the fact that you can't open a closet door without a landslide of no-longer-used (worthless?) items crashing down on you.

There's even a book out there called, *The Life-Changing Magic of Tidying Up*, which is all about organizing our stuff.

The book sold millions, has been translated into several languages, and was actually made into the Netflix series, *Tidying Up with Marie Kondo*. She was actually listed as one of Time's 100 most influential people in 2015. Her amazing success is all because we don't know how to say, "I already have enough stuff!" Imagine that! And let's not even get started on cable shopping networks that run 24/7 for the convenience of their viewers. Apparently all the stuff we once called "clutter" is now big business.

The point is that the stuff of this world consumes us and demands so much from us that it just makes sense to spend some time measuring its impact on our lives. Do we surf the web at all hours of the day and night looking for deals? Is our life merely a trivial pursuit to gather more stuff? Do we understand that one day our stuff will be on display in that antique mall? And most importantly of all, is it possible that the stuff we think we own, actually owns *us*?

Stuff in itself is not inherently evil. It is not wrong to work hard to provide for yourself and the ones you love. Scripture consistently sets forth that excelling in your chosen vocation is a good thing. In fact, God's Word says, *if anyone does not provide for his own, and especially for those of his household, he has denied the faith and is worse than an unbeliever* (1 Tim. 5:8). With your success comes varying degrees of reward and working hard and praying for your daily bread (Matt. 6:11) are good and honorable pursuits. Furthermore, it is not a sin to enjoy the things God has provided for you; however, selling your soul to gain the stuff that you think you can't live without might not only be unhealthy but extremely harmful as well. How you relate to, value, and manage all the stuff says a lot about who you are. It can shape you, and potentially define you.

The purpose of this book is not to deter you from your desires and ambitions, but to put your motivation into a framework; to lead you on a spiritual journey that can help you put all your stuff into its proper place. Taking the time to learn how the power of stuff can potentially control your life is time well invested. This book is about achieving balance between the material world and the eternal one. That is a big statement, but it is true. You, your family, your neighbors, and the faith communities you touch, desperately need you to manage wisely the stuff God has placed within your care.

So, for those of you courageous enough to go on a journey of self-discovery, I have some good news for you. It is possible to slay the dragon of materialism. I'm not saying that it will be easy to prevail, but I promise you it can be done. When you are born again, you become spiritually hard-wired by your Creator to find purpose in life in ways that transcend the tangible things that you see and desire.

Fearing what this will cost you will derail your transformation into the person God plans for you to become. Yes, it may appear at first that the cost of living a spiritually surrendered life is more than you want to pay. That's because your initial perception is tainted by a lifetime of focus on the false values of the temporal world around you. If you have the courage to take one step at a time toward a Christ-centered life, the fog will lift. You will recognize stuff for what it is as you begin to see temporary things as God sees them. You will see a whole other world you may not have seen before but know this: how you identify with the stuff that you can see, has much to do with the intangible spiritual world you can't see.

There are only a few reasons why you would dare to read a book so obviously focused on managing your personal belongings. You may have already awakened to the consequences of how your present "stuff management" practices aren't working. Or you may sense a stirring in your soul that is quietly whispering to you that there is more to life than just possessing another shiny thing. Maybe you were nudged by someone you care for, and out of respect, you find yourself reading a book you might not have picked up otherwise.

Regardless of the reason, if you have received Jesus into your life and if you allow God to transform your mind, you will see material things differently. Then your behavior will follow, and you will have the amazing opportunity to revolutionize your spending. You will become more like the One who saved you from your sins. Faithfully stewarding the possessions God has given you is the greatest life anyone can possibly live. You can have the opportunity to impact those who travel planet earth for a few short years of their physical life. Your new way of relating to all your stuff can potentially change the trajectory of another person's life in a way that will last for all eternity. I am honored to be your fellow traveler on this spiritual journey of understanding stuff.

—Ed

Yours, O Lord, is the greatness, the power, the glory, the victory, and the majesty. Everything in the heavens and on earth is yours, O Lord, and this is your kingdom. We adore you as the one who is over all things.

I CHRONICLES 29:11

CHAPTER ONE

Stuff — It can't make you happy

Those who love money will never have enough. How meaningless to think that wealth brings true happiness!

ECCLESIASTES 5:10

The hard truth about stuff is simple. It does not bring true happiness or lasting contentment. And yet, we spend much of our energy and time in pursuit of money to buy the stuff we are conditioned to believe we can't live without. Not realizing it, we become enslaved by stuff and if we don't resolve the true ownership issue, stuff starts to own us, even to unhealthy degrees.

We invest so much emotion into our belongings that instead of making us happy, one writer suggested that they may in fact drive us slightly mad.[1] Think about the hoarder who can't even throw out old food from the refrigerator, or the widow who hangs onto her late husband's belongings indefinitely. Others argue that possessions actually define who we are or that they are an extension of ourselves. It's a universal human trait that begins very early in life, such as the toddler declaring, "My blanket."[2]

The idea that you need *more* stuff to make you happy is a lie, a trap that imprisons you, rendering you unable to experience the real riches of life. The story is told of a wealthy man who was spurred on by overly self-centered behavior. Though he had much wealth, he still felt that he deserved more; but amid his upward ladder climb, he suffered a stroke and died. He believed that life without money was incomplete, but in the end, money without life was useless. Greed for more and more will rob you of the best things that life has to offer. You do not want to miss this warning, because your spiritual freedom and pathway to a fulfilled life are at stake.

Greed fuels the creative intellect of those who set aside all logic and long-standing moral values to do what they know to be wrong. Such was the case with slavery when the greed of slave owners ran headlong into their Christian faith. This is why Henry Ward Beecher, brother of *Uncle Tom's Cabin* author, Harriet Beecher Stowe, said, "All ambitions are lawful except those that climb upward on the miseries or credulities of mankind."[3] He was clearly exposing greed as the villain that blinded people to the evil of slavery.

In today's culture, greed could be defined as a disordered desire for more than is decent or deserved. Greed is totally based on one's self-interest, and while greed normally refers to money, it can also be a wanton desire for anything like food, power, status, attention, or even sex.[4]

King Solomon was considered to be a man wise above all others. That doesn't mean he was perfect, and I assure you that if you study Solomon's life, you will no doubt find flaws. About one subject however, he was always spot on – his wise writings about managing resources. As you read his words, think deeply about what Solomon wrote on the subject of greed in Proverbs, keeping in mind that his words are God-inspired. *If a bird sees a trap being set, it knows to stay away. But these people set an ambush for themselves; they are trying to get themselves killed. Such is the fate of all who are greedy for money; it robs them of life* (Prov. 1:17-19).

This passage points out another problem with greed. When you want more stuff than you need, you are setting in motion a series of events that will ensnare you and bring about your own demise. Greed for more stuff is consuming when your primary focus in life is driven by greed to get more. Then the moments that really matter will always get your second best. The drive to acquire more will leave little time for faith, family, and friends.

Greed is not something that only affects the rich. Virtually everyone is afflicted. When the unwealthy become victims of their own greed, hardly anyone notices beyond their own sphere of influence. But when the rich or famous are crushed by greedy ambition, you hear about it on the news. Wall Street investor Bernie Madoff, the mastermind behind the largest Ponzi scheme ever, became the poster child for the evil of greed.

When Madoff was finally caught after four decades of deception, it was determined his greed had driven him to rip off as much as 65 billion dollars. Although it has been difficult to ascertain the exact number of people he duped, it's possible that as many as 37,000 people fell victim to his greed. He was serving a 150-year prison sentence for investment fraud when he died in prison at the age of 82.[5] Madoff personified Proverbs 1:17-19 and quite obviously, *set an ambush* for himself. So much for greed. Certainly, his is a cautionary tale, but we can never forget that the same impulses that drove Bernie Madoff, are potentially in each and every one of us.

Take for example the easier to identify with story of greed like that of television stars Lori Laughlin and Felicity Huffman – two women who loved their kids and wanted to get them into prestigious schools. So, they cheated to move their children to the top of the pack, stealing admission spots from other, possibly more deserving applicants. The bribery scandal entrapped the schemers who faced prison time and who were also ordered to pay heavy fines.

Because we are all capable of being captured by greed, it is essential to understand that both the compulsion from within and the temptations from without precede our surrender to materialism. We live in a materialistic world that has conditioned us our whole lives to always want more stuff. There is a 24/7 bombardment of our minds calling upon us to consume. Television, radio, bloggers, social media influencers, online, offline, the world is screaming for us to buy, buy, buy! Add to all this the pressure we feel from our peers, and as we strive to "keep up with the Jones's," it all becomes a mind-numbing noise. This deafening roar of the world's marketing machine gets so loud you only faintly hear the voice within telling you to stop and bring balance to your life.

Fully aware of their ever-present power of persuasion, advertising companies spent an average of 6.5 million dollars for a 30-second ad during Super Bowl LVI.[6] These creative commercials stimulated us to buy everything from a new car to snack foods that weren't even good for us! The bottom line is that marketing works because it breaks down our logic and reason and appeals to our desire for more.

According to Statista, advertising expenditure in North America in 2021 amounted to about 297.5 billion U.S. dollars. This was a 19 percent increase from the year before. That breaks down to well over 700 dollars per person spent annually.[7] Being unaware of this systematic saturation of your mind will leave you vulnerable. So, how does one control the constant pressure to go after the next best thing?

Well, for one thing, you can limit the amount of time you spend surfing the internet for great deals. You might also try living within a reasonable budget or putting credit cards away if they are making "stuff-gathering" problematic. Realizing the potential problem with too much spending is most important, and as they say, to be forewarned is to be forearmed. Knowing the power of greed and the part it plays in temptation will help you recognize what is happening, especially when you start to make excuses for your actions. Remember, you are not alone in your struggles to reject the greedy impulse pushing you to obtain more stuff than you can afford or even need. God can help.

Because our human nature makes us vulnerable to greed, our Creator, the true and living God of this universe, gave us a command and set an absolute standard for us to obey. Going back 3,500 years ago, God spoke to Moses on Mt. Sinai and established a covenant agreement with His people. In a list commonly referred to as the Ten Commandments, the last commandment addresses this inherent trait in all people. It was established that God's people were never to look with greed at anything that another person had and desire to possess it. *You must not covet your neighbor's house. You must not covet your neighbor's wife, male or female servant, ox or donkey, or anything else that belongs to your neighbor* (Ex. 20:17). Thinking we must have something because someone else has it can be dangerous.

THE ORIGIN STORY OF STUFF AND GREED

Our propensity to be drawn to something that another person has, did not start with Moses's generation. The compulsion goes all the way back to the Garden of Eden. Adam and Eve clearly knew the forbidden fruit was not to be eaten or even touched. They had been told that the consequences of crossing the line would be death and still they disobeyed God. As a result, they became spiritually dead the moment they rejected God's command. What was the draw that compelled them to reject such a clear warning?

No doubt the answer to this question has many layers, but one thing is perfectly clear: Satan used the seductive power of visual attraction, coupled together with an appeal to their pride, to sell a taste of the forbidden fruit. The final blow to their obedience to God, was Satan's argument that caused Adam and Eve to doubt God's goodness. Satan convinced them that God was holding back something good. This temptation formula remains effective today, as Satan uses our basic greed against us, moving us to pursue the meaningless things that so often result in our demise. *The woman was convinced. She saw that the tree was beautiful, and its fruit looked delicious, and she wanted the wisdom it would give her. So, she took some of the fruit and ate it. Then she gave some to her husband, who was with her, and he ate it, too* (Gen. 3:6).

The Genesis account of Adam and Eve's surrender to the great deceiver's sales pitch, is followed by a series of cover up actions, which were intended to justify the rebellion of these first humans. They began by making a fig leaf covering for their newly discovered nakedness. Next, they hid from God when He came looking for them. Finally, they made excuses to deflect blame on each other.

But also found in the case of Adam and Eve, is the profound and wonderful truth of God's willingness to redeem them from their fall. God still sought them out and called for them. Even when they foolishly tried to hide from Him because they were ashamed of what they had done, God continued to love them. This is good news because we too have failed to heed God's warnings and in so many ways, have taken fruit that was never intended for us.

Just as God was willing to save Adam and Eve from their poor choices, and just as God provided an animal skin covering for the nakedness of those first sinners, a blood sacrifice through Jesus Christ offers us a covering for our sin. God's love is greater than any bad choice we have ever made concerning material things. No matter how much you have messed up, God is still calling for you to come to Him.

The idea that your financial decisions of where and how to spend your money is reflective of your spiritual condition, may be a new and even troubling concept to you. Yet, it is something you must be willing to consider. Just like Adam and Eve, we come face to face with the same sales pitch of the great deceiver. Satan deceives you with the fruit that is most attractive to you and then you cover up your actions with self-deception and self-serving justification.

Our only hope, our only way out of the maze of materialism and innate greed, is to follow the voice of the same God who came looking for Adam and Even in the Garden. His voice will lead you to spiritual peace and freedom from materialism. *For everything in the world, the lust of the flesh, the lust of the eyes, and the pride of life, comes not from the Father, but the world* (1 John 2:16 NIV).

We desperately need to come to terms with the truth about stuff. Even if you are successful in getting everything you think you want, the price is almost always too high as it was with Adam and Eve. You are missing out on eternal treasures that cannot be recovered, because you've invested in the things that can never last. Jesus put it this way: *And what do you benefit if you gain the whole world but lose your own soul?* (Mark 8:36)

When you look back in human history and see how people have allowed their pursuit of more stuff to destroy them, you gain insights that help you deal with the real-world issues regarding resource management. You grow in your capacity to look beyond the temptation of the present moment. You begin to see more clearly the value of investing in the eternal and understand how that leads to authentic joy. You can fulfill God's purpose for your life and ultimately experience true contentment, which is no small thing. In fact, Paul told his young protégé Timothy, that *godliness with contentment is in itself great wealth* (1 Tim. 6:6).

As a young parent I remember so clearly seeing something about myself in one of my own kids. It was one of those awareness moments when the light came on. My beautiful, innocent daughter had just grabbed a toy from another child and said, "mine." Though at the time I was stunned, I have long since realized that claiming everything as "mine" is very natural for an immature two-year-old. But the harsh and cruel reality is that as adults we too often behave much like immature two-year-olds. Cloaked in the cuteness of this story is the grim reality that as followers of Jesus we must grow up spiritually and act our age.

Spiritual growth requires spiritual food. A healthy diet of worship, consuming the Word of God, and selfless giving, leads us to be more like Jesus. As we live in Christ, we have the power to overcome this deeply imbedded obsession to have what other people have. So, beware! History has a way of repeating itself, which is a good reason to be very familiar with the origin story of stuff. We must overcome this drive to grab all that we can and stop saying, "it's mine."

STUFF HAS THE POWER TO OWN YOU

No one can serve two masters, for you will hate one and love the other; you will be devoted to one and despise the other. You cannot serve God and be enslaved to money.

MATTHEW 6:24

I remember the first time I really experienced the futility of allowing stuff to own me. My first car was a 1965 Ford

Mustang. Yep, it was an iconic Pony, which is now considered classic. When I was 16, it was just a used, four-year-old car that came to me needing a ton of repairs. The previous owner had put a fresh coat of paint and wax on the exterior and from the first moment I saw this Mustang, I just knew I had to make it mine.

But then, after I brought it home and parked it in my driveway, I noticed oil spots on the pavement that weren't there before. My dream car had some problems beneath the surface that I had been unwilling to see. Soon I discovered that the leaky oil was the least of my problems.

I was about to become a slave to my new car.

This shiny piece of happiness sitting in my driveway was a money pit. A new transmission, new clutch, new brakes, and a completely new exhaust system was just the beginning. Underneath the coat of new paint there soon emerged some flaking working its way through some poorly done body work. The rust would not be denied, and soon it was pushing its way to the surface.

The seller had failed to disclose that the car had been in a wreck, and replacement parts were far from what they should have been. I soon realized the car was out of alignment because the frame had been bent. It could not be fixed. It chewed up tires like a wild mustang would chew up an apple.

The choking control this car was having on my life started to feel like a noose around my neck.

I was now on the carousel of stuff, and I could not get off. One day while looking for parts in a football-field-sized junk yard of old rusted out cars, I realized something profound. Every broken-down car in that junk yard was at one time a bright shiny object, the stuff of someone's dreams. Now, as far as I could see, all that remained was junk. The shine was gone.

It is amazing how our dreams for shiny objects can so quickly become nightmares.

With my senior year of high school about to begin, I found myself in a quandary. I had already sunk all the money I had into "my freedom on wheels," but this hoped-for liberty was demanding more and more from me. What could I do?

I decided to double down. I picked up a part time job and sunk even more money into that V8, 289 cubic inches of Detroit power. Life was becoming a blur. Working on the car left little time for school, sports, church, or any of the other things a normal 17-year-old guy would hope to be doing his senior year of high school.

This saga eventually ended two years later between my freshman and sophomore years in college. That summer, working as an intern in a church in Tampa, Florida, I had to pour the entire summer's earnings into car repairs. I had been a slow learner, but the light was now flashing brightly, and I could ignore it no longer. It was time to rip off the band aid. I sold the car at a great financial loss, took a taxi to the airport, and flew back home. I was now wiser for the lessons I had learned about craving stuff that only rusts and decays. I was on a new path of freedom.

And what about you? Are you spending much of your time and effort repairing your broken-down stuff? Could it be that too much of your life is driven by a pursuit for more? If you see even a little of yourself in the lesson I learned from my Mustang, then you are ready to look beyond the glitter of stuff and discover that there is something more meaningful in life than chasing temporal things. Obviously, we need a certain amount of stuff to live, but if greed is driving the pursuit of more and more stuff, it has all your attention and time, and you will miss out on all the things that matter the most. Proverbs 15:17 tells us *better a small serving of vegetables with love than a fattened calf with hatred* (NIV). Stuff cannot buy the best things in life like the bond of family, the warm embrace of loved ones, the sound of children laughing, or the confidence that you have lived your best life. Maybe it's time to see the value in that *small serving of vegetables* instead of recklessly spending for things that are harmful to you. Maybe it's time to see that less is actually more.

When our drive to secure more things becomes stronger than our love for people, we have bowed before the god of materialism. That word is defined as the preoccupation with or emphasis on material objects, comforts, and considerations with a disinterest in or a rejection of spiritual, intellectual, or cultural values. Now compare that to 1 John 2:15: *Do not love this world nor the things it offers you, for when you love the world, you do not have the love of the Father in you.*

Jesus told us that the two greatest commandments were to love God and love others. (See Matthew 22:37-39). We know that God loves His followers, but He loves the rest of the world as well. So, if you have a loving relationship with God, your willingness to love people more than stuff actually proves your love for Him. It is His purpose and our privilege to pay God's love forward. The Apostle John shared many spiritual insights with us on this subject. He said, *if someone has enough money to live well and sees a brother or sister in need but shows no compassion—how can God's love be in that person?* (1 John 3:17). He restated this thought in the next chapter by saying, *He who does not love, does not know God, for God is love* (1 John 4:8). When we focus on the people and things that God loves, instead of personal greed and selfish wants, we have changed our focus from temporal spending to eternal investing.

Mother Theresa, who sacrificed worldly things and invested her life in loving others, said, "Today, if we have no peace, it is because we have forgotten that we belong to each other – that man, that woman, that child is my brother or my sister."[8] We have a responsibility to love and care for others, but if we are completely consumed with accumulating more stuff for our own pleasure, we are incapable of loving others as God would have us do.

Some people have known nothing but want and need their entire lives while others are immersed in privilege and opportunity. But regardless of financial standing, we are instructed to help those in need, and we are completely unable to do that unless we make peace with our attitudes and values about spending it all on ourselves. Changing or prioritizing our values is a journey we each must take with God's help. Your circumstances are not exclusive to you, but they are exclusively yours. No matter where you came from, God wants to lead you forward and bring you to that place of compassion that is possible despite the challenges you face in this materialistic world.

The journey simplified is this: You have been created to know God's love and to love Him back. Then through experiencing His love, you in turn love others. That is the only way to put the value of temporary worldly things into its proper place.

The purpose of this book is not to suggest that you swear an oath of poverty and live the life of an impoverished 12th century monk. Poverty alone, is not in and of itself a reflection of godliness. Nor is wealth evidence of an evil heart. In fact, many of the wealthiest people in scripture, such as Job, Solomon, or Abraham, were some of the most spiritually honorable. But I assure you, if you dare to read on, you will discover how to measure the values of the temporal world against the spiritual values of the eternal world. You will know how to be rich in the things that matter regardless of how much money you have.

Many will dismiss the idea that eternal values drive God's economy, because they believe it will cost them too much. They believe the way to live a happy and satisfying life is to hold onto what they have while pursuing even more stuff. These are people who convince themselves that churches, charities, or someone in the community who needs help only wants their money. I'm sure that's true in some situations, but I still believe that most pastors and spiritual leaders are sincerely more concerned with the hurts and needs of those who cannot help themselves.

No matter what your excuse or reasoning may be, if you avoid realigning your values with eternal spiritual values, you may leave this world with more stuff in your toybox than others, but you will enter eternity naked and broke. According to the book of Ecclesiastes, life and everything in it is a meaningless vapor, because it is all here today and gone tomorrow. James compared life to a morning fog. *Here a little while and then it's gone* (James 4:14). You may choose to grab everything you can in your brief life, meanwhile missing out on some of the greatest blessings that exist when you choose people over stuff. But saddest of all, you will not have fulfilled the purpose that God designed for you.

Not My Stuff is more about the condition of your heart than the balance in your bank account. It is about aligning what you value with what God values. It is about how you are investing your life. And it is important to note, that in the timeless economy of our Creator, your optimum spiritual condition can be achieved regardless of whether you were born rich or poor or anyplace in between. This is the real truth about stuff and stewardship.

Your challenge now is to dig deep and get honest about the things you truly love and value in life. This will no doubt be a challenging journey because one does not transform a long-held way of thinking and living without some soulful struggling. But putting the material world into an eternal perspective transforms your mind and eventually your life. A truly meaningful life is possible when you see the material things of this world and are able to honestly say, "it is not my stuff!"

Let God transform you into a new person by changing the way you think.

ROMANS 12:2

WHAT DOES KNOWING THE TRUTH ABOUT STUFF LOOK LIKE?

I have seen joy and contentment in the most unlikely of places. In August 1986, Kathy and I moved to South Florida where I had been called to serve as the lead pastor of a church. On our first Sunday there, we were invited to dinner at the home of an elderly charter member of the church. One of the first things I noticed upon our arrival to her home was that the windows of the small, humble home were open, and I heard the sound of old box fans humming. With the hot Florida sun looming directly above, I was concerned. It was nearly 100 degrees in the shade on this August day in South Florida, so surely our host had air-conditioning, right?

This was a serious question to me. I was from northern Ohio where summers were cool, and where lots of folks lived without AC. But now we were in Florida, and I was wondering how anyone could live without the cool benefits of central air in a place where you could literally fry an egg on the sidewalk! I guess I was about to find out, and soon my host Nettie, would teach me some things about stuff and about what was really important in life.

My family and I took our seats around a table which was covered with a hand-stitched quilted tablecloth. The table was very small with barely enough room for our plates. The silverware did not match, and no two glasses were alike, although a couple of the mason jars were the same. I don't think I could have anticipated how my heart (as well as my stomach) would soon be filled. We were about to feast on the sweet truth of how Nettie saw life and what mattered most to her.

She was a salt of the earth woman from the Appalachian Mountains of Kentucky, a strong independent and self-sufficient widow in her late 80's. I hate to even admit it now, but she reminded me of the Granny character on the TV show, *The Beverly Hillbillies*. She welcomed us in and made us feel right at home, in fact she made us feel like family.

As we talked, she expressed her thankfulness to God for answering her prayers and bringing the new young pastor to the church. By now, I had shed a layer of my Sunday clothes, and I found myself forgetting about our humble surroundings. My family was dining with one of the most remarkable, unpretentious, and contented women I'd ever met – a child of God who believed herself to be rich, who gave thanks for her daily bread, and freely shared it with others. She was living out her faith and valuing people more than stuff.

On that memorable hot summer day, it was clear, stuff did not own my host, nor was she enamored by the things of this world. She had migrated to Florida, before I was even born with little more than the clothes she was wearing. But when the church needed funds for a new building, Nettie was the first to respond, rivaling the widow woman of Luke 21 with her giving. She chose to see the stuff God had given her as enough and was content. For many years thereafter, she taught me more and more truth about stuff by her example. Stuff did not own her; it did not control her. She lived a peaceful, contented life and was a blessing to others until God called her home where she now enjoys the rewards she had sent ahead, because she truly understood the truth about stuff and what it meant to be God's steward.

CHAPTER TWO

Ownership — It's all God's stuff

Everything in the heavens and on earth is yours, O Lord, and this is your kingdom. We adore you as the one who is over all things.

1 CHRONICLES 29:11

In one of my earliest battles with the ownership issue, once again a car was involved. It happened at a time when I needed more reliable transportation. As a young pastor, it seemed that I was spending more time fixing my car than I was using it to do the work of ministry. Hospital visits, funerals, weddings, and going to home Bible studies all required a reliable vehicle. So, after much prayer and research, I made the decision to get another car, faithfully concluding that the new car would not really be mine, it would belong to God. After purchasing the car and driving out of the car lot, I even began saying out loud to myself, "This is God's car." (I had to keep reminding myself to practice what I preach!)

Little by little, however, the lines began to blur when it came down to the car's real owner. Because I was the one driving the car, it was easy to forget who really owned it. The first Sunday I drove it to church, I parked in a seldom-used area toward the back of the parking lot, telling myself that I was saving the premium parking closest to the church for the guests and the elderly. But the truth was, I was already sliding back into self-ownership, and I didn't want anyone to ding the door of *my* new car.

Less than ten minutes before it was time for me to preach, a man came running to the front of the church with a horrified look in his eyes. My first thought was that it must be an emergency, or he wouldn't have disturbed me so close to the start of the service. Turns out it was a catastrophe of epic proportions! Someone had driven to that secluded space of supposed safety and crashed into *my* new car.

I took a deep breath and said to those around me, "I'm not upset, I'm not mad." After all, the car was not mine, right? When I rather smugly and piously said those words, I think I was trying to convince myself that I really did believe what I was saying. I remember thinking, this is not a problem, this is God's car. So out loud, one more time for effect, I added,

"Really, I'm not mad, but I'm pretty sure *God* is mad that someone just crashed into *His* car." I walked into the pulpit that day prepared to preach about God's love, but honestly, I was angry and felt more like preaching on God's wrathful vengeance toward those who destroy His possessions! I'm ashamed as I look back because I know my attachment to that car, a material thing, was overshadowing my belief that it was God's property in the first place. I confessed my fault, hugged the young man who hit the car and never looked back. God used the entire incident to teach me a life-long lesson that He is the *One who is over all things,* and I am only the steward.

A steward is someone entrusted to manage resources that belong to someone else. Jesus explained that *A faithful, sensible servant is one to whom the master can give the responsibility of managing his other household servants and feeding them. If the master returns and finds that the servant has done a good job, there will be a reward. I tell you the truth, the master will put that servant in charge of all he owns* (Matt. 24:45-47).

As the verse tells us, when this trust is faithfully carried out, there is great reward. But when anyone chooses to use God's material blessings yet fails to affirm His rightful ownership, they will ultimately lose everything.

Jesus preached selflessness to the crowds when He said, *If any of you wants to be my followers, you must turn from your selfish ways…If you try to hang on to your life, you will lose it. But if you give up your life for my sake and for the sake of the Good News, you will save it* (Matt. 16:24-25). Many people spend their entire lives seeking pleasure and worldly things, but Jesus wants us to choose to follow His goals rather than live a life of self-gratification. He summed up this lesson with a thought-provoking question, *What do you benefit if you gain the whole world but lose your own soul?* (verse 26).

That is a relevant question. If you use all the things that God has blessed you with for self-gratification and worldly gain, you have in reality wasted His provisions, because what you gain here on earth will be lost forever in eternity. So, either you acknowledge that God owns everything and manage His resources responsibly, or you spend your life in conflict with the True Owner of everything in the heavens and earth. You can't just say, "God owns all the stuff" and then fail to recognize His ownership by managing His stuff for your own personal pleasure. Our stewardship practices either affirm or deny His ownership.

Resolving ownership issues is easier said than done. For example, years ago there was a bumper sticker that said, "Honk if you love Jesus." That was followed by a bumper sticker that said, "Tithe if you love Jesus, anyone can honk." The old saying, "talk is cheap," seems appropriate when it comes to issues of stewardship, because our actions do speak so much louder than our words.

Buying into the belief that God owns it all is a struggle that will take some time. There is no switch to throw, no contract to sign that seals the deal. It is a matter of daily surrender to the Owner of the stuff. More than anything else, it is about our personal relationship with the Owner. Growing closer to God, allows us to affirm His ownership authentically. This struggle is never over, and the journey never reaches the finish line until we stand before God one day absent from the restraints of our physical bodies and selfish human desires. Until then, there is a powerful truth to embrace every day of our lives that makes all the difference in the world, and that is Divine Ownership.

WHAT IS DIVINE OWNERSHIP?

Divine Ownership is an absolute truth acknowledging that God, the Creator of all, is also the Owner of all. He owns our bodies, our finances and possessions, our talents, the 24 hours in our day, and the very air that we breathe. Everything. We are simply caretakers who get to use and appropriate the blessings He gives. From the first recorded account in human history, God has required mankind to watch over the world that He created. This was always His plan. *The Lord God placed the man in the Garden of Eden to tend and watch over it* (Gen. 2:15).

The Garden of Eden was a perfect environment, complete with everything Adam and Eve could ever want. God provided all of it, and in return all they had to do was take care of it. There was only one stipulation. God made clear to them that there was one fruit in the center of the garden that was off limits. Soon, however, a deceiver named Satan tempted them into believing that God was depriving them of something, so what did they do? They desired the one thing that God said they could not have and consumed it themselves. That disregard for God's instructions about the ownership of that fruit was a serious offense, and since the fall of Adam and Eve, their selfish desire to claim what is God's has passed to all humanity.

When we tightly clutch the things that belong to God and call it our own, we are in rebellion against Him. Because of this conflict I would argue that you can't even fully enjoy or even appreciate the stuff you have until you affirm God's Divine Ownership. Solomon said that it's meaningless to think that worldly possessions and wealth can bring true happiness, because in reality the only thing it does is *slip through your fingers* (Eccl. 5:11). The truth is, you can't take your riches with you, which is why they say you'll never see a U-Haul attached to a hearse.

So, the only question is whether you will accept your role of being a wise steward of all that He owns or claim it for yourself. Because He created us with capable minds and bodies, it is only logical to assume that even the ability to acquire wealth in the first place is a God-given gift, so you should be mindful to use your possessions and resources to fulfill His kingdom work. It is remarkable when you think about it. You have been given the privilege of caring for the things that belong to God and using them for furthering His kingdom as well.

Being a steward and caring for something of value is captured in the advertising campaign of the extremely costly Patek Philippe wristwatch. Their slogan is, "You never actually own a Patek Philippe. You merely look after it for the next generation."[1] This add is usually accompanied by a photo representing a father/son portrait. With limitations, this watch company has fallen onto something important. In a very real way, no one owns anything, and in the case of the stuff of the world, all of it belongs to God, and all that we *think* we possess will be passed on to someone else.

In Matthew 25:14-30, Jesus helps us understand Divine Ownership with the Parable of the Three Servants. In this story a man of wealth went on a long trip, but before going away, he called his three servants together and entrusted bags of gold and silver to them, dividing it according to their abilities. Upon his return, the master discovered that two of his servants had invested and even multiplied the bags of gold they had been given. The master was full of praise! They celebrated together, and the master promised to give the wise stewards even more. The third servant who turned out to be a very poor steward, had hidden the gold. He had not used it for the master's good purposes and was therefore called wicked and lazy and was then cast out. The lesson of this parable is found in verse 29, *To those who use well what they are given, even more will be given, and they will have an abundance. But from those who do nothing, even what little they have will be taken away.*

Over the last four decades I was blessed with the privilege of being a local church pastor. During that time, I made many sobering observations regarding the way people view and treat stuff. The ones who understand that 100 percent of all they possess belongs to God in the first place, are clearly happier than those who live their lives scratching and clawing to get more.

An on-line article entitled *Givers Really Are Happier Than Takers*, revealed that "even small acts of generosity trigger a brain boost."[2] Studies show that generosity is rewarding and that "the brain is seemingly hardwired for happiness in response to giving."[3] While that may leave scientists stumped, it's no surprise to us because we know who hardwired the brain.

So, it seems that being a giver has a positive effect on a person's life. They have deeper relationships, better physical and mental health, a more positive outlook on life, are happier in their careers, and tend to be more satisfied with what they have.[4]

Believers of Divine Ownership who are givers are others-centered while takers are self-centered. They fail to recognize God's ownership over all things and live with the false perception that the stuff belongs to them, and that using the stuff for themselves will make them happy. They fall short of their spiritual potential because of their wrong thinking and short-sightedness, missing out on opportunities God gives to invest in people whose lives can be changed eternally.

A total surrender to God and the truth of Divine Ownership is the first step in your journey toward becoming the faithful steward God intends you to be. You don't have to be rich to be a faithful steward of God's stuff. You are only required to humbly accept His plan and purpose for your life. It is a liberating moment when you can look around at everything you see and are able to declare, "It is not *my* stuff." Once you see that you were intended to be a steward of God's stuff, you step into a life of courageous faith.

Divine Ownership is a spiritual issue, a matter of the heart. Your spiritual growth and well-being are reflected in the way you carry out your stewardship responsibilities. Becoming a good steward is difficult because there are always competing emotions pulling in opposite directions, but few things in life will have greater reward than when you choose to manage God's resources wisely. Being a good steward does not make you a good Christian but being a good Christian will make you a good steward.

That desire to have more and more for ourselves directly conflicts with our desire to please and honor God. But a good steward's life is filled with meaning and purpose. They recognize that God has given them resources so that they in turn can, not only meet their own needs, but bless others as well. They are people who see the world as God sees it, and are able to help others in God's family, and also love the spiritually unresolved by investing in ways that bring the Good News to them. These life-impacting activities are not possible until you first filter the stuff you previously called your own, through the truth of who really owns it.

There is no way to sugar coat the challenges you will face by choosing God over all the stuff.

Perhaps all you have ever known is the idea that the stuff you possess really is yours. And why not? A lifetime of experiences reinforces that belief. The money in the bank account has your name on it; the car is titled in your name; the place where you live is your personal address. It takes a complete reprogramming of your mind to revise such a world view, because it is just not natural to fully grasp the concept that God actually owns everything you have. But failing to see this truth exposes selfishness and rebellion as the heart's true condition.

JESUS AND DIVINE OWNERSHIP

Mark 10:17-31 tells of a rich young man who asked Jesus what he needed to do to have eternal life. He explained to Jesus that he was a good man and always kept the Ten Commandments. Because Jesus knew that it is possible to do good things and still close your heart to God, He offered the man a challenge. Jesus told him to sell everything he had, give all the money to the poor, and follow Him. The man walked away deeply troubled because his earthly possessions were many. The issue for Jesus, was not that someone had to give all their wealth to enter Heaven, but that they needed to give all of their heart.

The rich young man was unable to do that, so he chose to live rich and die poor.

In this story you can see that what Jesus told the rich man troubled His closest followers. They pressed Jesus and asked how anyone could go to heaven if the bar was so high that it required a person to give everything away. But in this passage it is clear that Jesus never wanted the man to sell everything, He just knew how difficult it was for the wealthy to break free from enslavement to their possessions, and so He said, *It is easier for a camel to go through the eye of a needle than for a rich person to enter the Kingdom of God!* (Mark 10:25). This statement by Jesus helps us understand the real issue. This rich man believed his possessions belonged to him and he was not willing to surrender ownership to God. He was wrong about what matters the most.

I want to say it again, the issue is not how much money you give, but how much of your heart you give to God. The lessons in this story are so important that Matthew, Mark, and Luke were all compelled to record the same encounter with the rich man. God inspired these writers to repeat this conversation to stress that God does not want just parts of our lives and possessions, but He wants our all. It is so clear that at the heart of the story is the principle of Divine Ownership.

Who knows how this story would have ended if the man had humbly surrendered all that he had. We will never know for sure, but it could have played out much like Abraham's encounter with God when he too was asked to make an unthinkable sacrifice. When Abraham by faith trusted God and His goodness enough to surrender the life of his only son, God intervened and told him that he would not be required to make this sacrifice. That's because all God ever wanted was for Abraham to willingly trust Him with all that he had, even his precious son, Isaac.

Oh, to be more like Abraham who passed the test of faith with flying colors. Instead, too often we have more in common with the man who struggled to give all. Why is it so difficult to give our hearts to Him completely? Why is it so challenging to make Jesus Christ Lord of everything in our lives?

An article I read asked, "What kind of welcome has Jesus received in the entryway of your heart? Is He more like family or is He only a guest?"[5] The writer goes on to say that if we don't love Jesus with all our heart, soul, strength, and mind, the best thing we can do is admit it and open the door wide and invite Him in to make us whole. Sounds like the perfect plan to me. As I've said, our unwillingness to embrace God's ownership of our lives and everything we have is really an indication of what's going on in our hearts. Failure to completely surrender to God is evidence that the stuff of this world matters more to us than God.

DIVINE OWNERSHIP THE PUREST MOTIVE FOR GIVING

The surrender of our hearts and our motives is very important. One thing that separates New Testament Christianity from almost every other religion is that our heart relationship with God is more important than good deeds. In other words, the inner condition of the heart holds greater value than actions. The reason being is that our actions or behaviors flow forth from the heart's condition. God cares about what we do, but even more importantly, He cares *why* we do these things. He's interested in the secret part of our heart that is hidden from the eyes of others who know us and see what we are doing.

In the first century, following the death and resurrection of Jesus, the new churches in Macedonia exemplified what pure motives looked like. Even though they themselves were in great poverty and under severe persecution, they willingly sent funds to help the starving church in Jerusalem. In his letter to the Corinthian church, Paul wrote, *Now I want you to know, dear brothers and sisters, what God in his kindness has done through the churches in Macedonia. They are tested by many troubles, and they are very poor. But they are also filled with abundant joy, which has overflowed in rich generosity* (2 Cor. 8:1-2). These churches were happy to give so that their poverty-stricken brothers and sisters living in famine could receive lifesaving relief. Their pure motives compelled them to give for all the right reasons. Their hearts were filled with gratitude and an awareness that they owed the entirety of their lives to God. They had seen God work and knew He was real.

In contrast to pure giving, there are other reasons that people give that do not receive God's favor. One such false motive is **giving to get**. These folks feel that after giving to their church, God is *obligated* to give them back more money than they gave. I wish I could tell you that there is a magic formula guaranteeing that your tithes and offerings would always put money back in your pocket, but God never made such a promise. To think so is absurd and requires you to take scripture out of context.

In Luke 6:38 when Jesus told the crowd *give, and you will receive,* He wasn't promising them a monetary guarantee, nor was He saying that their dividends would be seen on earth. It's true that many times we *do* reap the rewards of giving here on earth, but Jesus had just told His disciples in verse 23 of that chapter that their rewards were in heaven. So, the benefits of giving as God commanded can't be measured in a bank account, because the riches of an obedient child of God, surrendered to Divine Ownership, are measured in eternal currency. We should never be motivated to give by hoping for personal gain. We give because we love God and others, and because He has given so much to us.

Another flawed reason to give is the **angry God threat**. This is the belief that God in His anger will bring plagues of destruction into your life if you fail to honor Him with your finances. I will admit that the idea of an angry God just waiting to zap a non-giver appeals to me as a pastor! Wouldn't it be nice to teach that motive with a clear conscience and scare people into giving? No, that's really not a good plan at all. It might increase the church offering in the short term, but it is a terrible long-term path to follow because that idea does not come from a heart of love. Fear of what will happen to you if you don't give to God, cannot mold you into a spiritually healthy person like the principle of Divine Ownership can.

Guilt is another flawed reason for giving. I have seen guilt used in many ways to nudge people toward their wallets. Some churches go so far as to send a finance committee member to peoples' homes with a hard ask for a designated amount to help meet the church budget goals, leaving the manipulated church member feeling personally responsible for keeping the church doors open. This method robs individuals of joyful giving and ultimately leads to bitterness.

By contrast, giving to causes and things that are close to God's heart brings the fullness of God's peace.

Finally, **pride** makes our list of top poor reasons to give. In Acts chapter five, we see the first century Christians bringing their offerings to the apostles to help their poor persecuted brothers and sisters in Christ. These offerings were not mandated or required but given from generous hearts with pure motives. Enter Ananias and Saphira who brought their gift to Peter, and pridefully exaggerated the amount, claiming to have sold property and that they were giving *all* the proceeds to their church. It wasn't necessary to lie, but they wanted to look good in front of others. As a result, they missed out on the blessing and died instead!

Consider this warning from Matthew 6:1-4:

> *Watch out! Don't do your good deeds publicly, to be admired by others, for you will lose the reward from your Father in heaven. When you give to someone in need, don't do as the hypocrites do - blowing trumpets in the synagogues and streets to call attention to their acts of charity! I tell you the truth, they have received all the reward they will ever get. But when you give to someone in need, don't let your left hand know what your right hand is doing. Give your gifts in private, and your Father who sees everything, will reward you.*

Fear, guilt, greed, pride, and any other false motivation for giving will never allow you to fully experience the real joy of generosity that comes from a heart that loves God and desires to please Him. Long-term, heartfelt spiritual health matures most completely when you act out of loving obedience for the One who loved you and gave His life to save you from your sin.

DIVINE OWNERSHIP'S CONNECTION TO SPIRITUAL GROWTH

The spiritual journey is a life-long process. We begin as babes in Christ but grow and mature to become more like Jesus. The process is never really over until we leave this world and the limitations of our fleshly bodies behind. As spiritually committed as the Apostle Paul was, he openly admitted that even after years of following Jesus he was still not where he wanted to be. *I don't mean to say that I have already achieved these things or that I have already reached perfection. But I press on to possess that perfection for which Christ Jesus first possessed me* (Phil. 3:12).

Paul's words ring true for each of us, for none of us has reached perfection in our relationship with God through Jesus Christ. No one escapes the daily struggle between our selfish human desires and what we want to do spiritually. But when with each struggle, we make the right choice to trust and follow God, we have in that moment taken one step closer to becoming more like Christ. This process of spiritual growth is possible because of the power of God's grace, but it is a journey of ups and downs, forward and backward motion.

John Newton, a former captain of slave ships, went from profiting from the brutality of slavery to being an outspoken 18th century abolitionist in Great Britain. The man who wrote the words to possibly the most famous hymn in the last 300 years knew first-hand what God's *Amazing Grace* was all about. After he was converted to Christianity, he would not only renounce the slave trade but invest much of the rest of his life seeking to outlaw the evil practice. When asked about his past sins, he is to have said, "I am not what I ought to be, I am not what I want to be, I am not what I hope to be in another world; but still I am not what I once used to be, and by the grace of God I am what I am."[6]

It is doubtful that anyone reading this book has the blood of others on their hands like the former slave trader, but we have all experienced setbacks in our Christian journey. We have all done things we wish we could undo, because we all struggle with obedience to God. And because we all live in flawed human bodies it's necessary to get up every day and take another step closer to Jesus through personal times of prayer, worship, and reading of scripture. Accountability through our local church relationships is also helpful in the journey. This maturing process is essential, and in spite of taking three steps forward and two steps back, the work of redemption that Jesus began in your life will be completed by the power of God. *And I am certain that God, who began the good work within you, will continue his work until it is finally finished on the day when Christ Jesus returns* (Phil. 1:6).

God's power in your life makes it possible for the impossible to happen. If you have been *born again* (John 3:5-7), the power to become more like Jesus is already part of your life in the person of His Holy Spirit. He will empower you to do what you might think is impossible, including living your life within the truth of Divine Ownership. God is working in your life right now, and even reading this book about giving back to God is proof that you desire to be more obedient. You may even experience some angst and fear about turning possessions over to Him, but please read on and trust that God has something wonderful in store for you. And when you begin to see God do the impossible in your life and with your finances, you will one day look back and wonder why you ever doubted.

DIVINE OWNERSHIP MAKES
WORSHIPFUL GIVING POSSIBLE

Open my eyes to see the wonderful truths in your instructions.

PSALM 119:18

Misunderstanding the truth about Divine Ownership blinds us to a significant focus of the Christian faith, causing us to misinterpret what we hear any time the subject of money is raised at church (or for that matter, any other time the issue comes up). If you only hear a plea for money, you miss the true purpose of worshipful giving.

- The true purpose for giving is not to finance another building for the church. The purpose of the building is to provide a place for God's people to worship, grow in God's truth, and to be the Church when we go out into the world.

- The true purpose of giving is not merely to pay the salary of the church staff. The true purpose of providing for the needs of the people in vocational ministries is to advance the mission of the Church by making it possible for those called by God to serve full time.

- The true purpose of giving is not just to fund the church budget. The purpose of worshipful giving allows a church to budget for all the costs associated with providing a place for worship, growth, and for equipping people to carry out the mission Jesus gave His Church.

All these things just listed are true, but you must understand the true purpose of giving an offering to the Lord, is to acknowledge that everything belongs to Him, and in so doing give Him the glory He deserves. It is only then that you can truly enter into His presence and worship because you are acting on the foundational truth about God's ownership. *Give to the Lord the glory he deserves. Bring your offering and come into his presence. Worship the Lord in all his holy splendor* (1 Chron. 16:29).

CHALLENGES TO DIVINE OWNERSHIP

Challenging God about ownership issues and trying to wrestle His stuff away from Him, creates a state of feuding. You might remember the story of the feud between the Appalachian families, the Hatfield's and McCoy's. In 1878, Floyd Hatfield and Randolph McCoy began a prolonged conflict that began because of their disagreement over the ownership of some pigs.

Supposedly, the pigs wandered from the McCoy's farm onto the property of the Hatfield's who then claimed the pigs as their own. The case ended up before the local justice of the peace who happened to be a relative of the Hatfield clan, giving the case little chance of being fair and impartial. The Hatfield judge ruled that the pigs belonged to his relatives because of an old legal opinion that "possession is nine-tenths of the law." The feud escalated over two decades resulting in the tragic loss of life for both families. Either consciously or subconsciously, this bizarre logic enters into the opinion of many today who think they own God's stuff just because it has wandered onto their property.

We think because the stuff is "on our property," it must be ours. Some people will spend their entire lives feuding with God in this conflict, but they can never win. Tragically, because of disobedience, they may never realize all the wonderful things He intended for them; but obedient and surrendered children of God fulfill His purposes and experience priceless privileges and blessings.

The heart of God must be broken when so many who claim the name of Christ, seem to be ignoring the spiritual truth of Divine Ownership when they love stuff more than Him and this spiritually needy world. I'm not suggesting that we all take a vow of poverty or embrace a calling like Mother

Teresa. I am simply saying that we are all called upon to manage the resources in our care with a love for God and His plan. It is no exaggeration to say that resources for God's eternal purposes are desperately needed but in short supply.

Perhaps you find the concept of God's ownership too challenging and are already listing all the reasons why this just won't work for you. You think it impossible. Two centuries ago, there was a man named Charles Thomas Studd, who spent his life in dedicated service to God as a missionary to China. He once said, "Christ wants *not* nibblers of the possible, but grabbers of the impossible by faith in the omnipotence, fidelity, and wisdom of the Almighty Savior." It's not surprising that before his death, he also penned the words, "Only one life, t'will soon be past, only what's done for Christ will last."[7]

The obsession to own more stuff has many names. Greed, materialism, narcissism, self-love, and vanity to name a few. Paul reminded us in Philippians chapter two that we should stop trying to impress everyone but look to the needs and interests of others. Selfish living is contrary to having the mind of Christ and is a life that rejects Divine Ownership.

It would be wonderful to say that all Christians and church attenders practice Divine Ownership, but such is not the case. Rejecting Divine Ownership, and prioritizing things above God, is like trying to serve two masters. Jesus made it perfectly clear that no one can do that successfully. *For you will hate one and love the other; you will be devoted to one and despise the other. You cannot serve God and be enslaved to money* (Luke 16:13).

Some people dismiss Divine Ownership because they credit *themselves* for acquiring all their worldly possessions. Rather than having a grateful heart to God for His blessings, they assume they have done it all themselves and therefore, God has no claim to those possessions. Claiming ownership of everything that is God's is also tempting when individuals don't believe they will be held accountable for claiming God's things as their own. For a while it may seem they are getting away with misappropriating His resources, but God's law of sowing and reaping says otherwise.

THE BOTTOM LINE OF DIVINE OWNERSHIP

It seems that many Christians suffer from an addiction to stuff. Their giving or lack thereof, proves what they love the most. If you want to do the math for yourself, all you must do is calculate the number of people who attend a church and compare that to the generosity reflected in that church's giving. The math does not add up, and the bottom line is hard to ignore, that sadly, most people who claim to be Christians are not givers. Here are just a few general observations about Christian charity that will help give clarity to the state of the church's obedience to God's Divine Ownership plan.

- Only 5% of people who attend church regularly give 10% or more of their income.
- Of the 247 million people in the U.S. who identity as Christians, only 1.5 million give a tithe which is 10% of their income.
- If every Christian tithed, faith organizations would have an extra 139 billion dollars each year.[8]

Statistics, however, do not tell the whole story, they merely give us a place to start as we attempt to measure how Christians respond to Jesus's teachings on stewardship. It is not my purpose to be a prophet of condemnation or doom and despair, but to help us see the potential that exists for the Church if we all became willing stewards of God's possessions.

Because giving is an extremely private and personal matter, how much you give, where to give, and when to give should be determined in the privacy of your heart. No one should judge another person's giving – that's not part of our role as stewards. Only God knows the true intent of a person's heart, and if we attempt to figure out who is falling short of God's plan, we will certainly get it wrong. According to Jesus, a woman in poverty who gave the least was by God's standard, giving the most. *Jesus called his disciples to him and said, 'I tell you the truth, this poor widow has given more than all the others who are making contributions'* (Mark 12:43).

So, the real issue is never how much you give but how much you have left after you give. Before we finish this study, we will thoughtfully and carefully cover the issues that help you determine how much to give and even where God may be leading you to give. This will allow you to be certain that you are wisely investing God's money in areas closest to His heart.

DIVINE OWNERSHIP, THE FOUNDATION OF FINANCIAL PLANNING

Once you embrace Divine Ownership, you can be confident that God will help you determine how to manage the resources that He has entrusted to you. With God's help you can figure out how much to use for you and your family, as well as how much to give. Although the main focus of this book is not to equip you in preparing a budget or guide your financial planning, it is still essential that you take seriously your responsibility to manage God's resources well. Perhaps ask a church leader to recommend a study or workshop on the subject of God's plan for your personal finances, with a focus on making and managing a budget that is specific to your individual or family's needs. We are to use, not abuse, the resources He has given us. The truth is, in most cases, problems with giving begin with a mismanagement of what we've already been blessed with. Overspending on non-essentials is the destroyer of many budgets. Often, we put ourselves in a position of not being able to give because we are overextended by our own excess.

I have noticed that when people try to explain why they do not give, it almost always has to do with their perception that they can't afford to give. The excuses for not giving go away when you manage resources wisely. More money will not solve your financial problems if you don't know the difference between wants and needs (an issue we will cover in a later chapter). Waste, bad habits, and addictions will undo the best of intentions; but spiritual discipline and a plan will set you free.

As we have already discussed, strongly believing that everything belongs to God comes through a process of spiritual growth. Each step you take as you grow, adds another brick to the solid foundation that stands firm and guards against wanting more stuff. Building into your daily life an affirmation of the Divine Ownership commitment helps keep you on track. You will be well on your way to overcoming the seduction of seeing something and wanting to possess it as your own.

THE DIVINE OWNERSHIP BREAKTHROUGH

There is only one antidote to the greed epidemic and that is Jesus. Only Jesus, who left the glory of heaven to die for the sins of the world, can help you overcome the allure for material things. Those who practice Divine Ownership, bear witness to the fact that once Jesus fills a person's life, there is no longer space for stuff to control. Loving unselfishly, serving sacrificially, and giving generously now rule and define their lives.

God has a plan for His people and His Church. Nothing asked of us in scripture is unattainable, and for every command or mission, given to the Church, there is a solution built into the life we are called to lead. The Great Commission in Matthew 28, to go into all the world, is completely possible when Christians choose the life of faithfully stewarding everything in their care. God never asks us to do anything that He has not already made a provision for. His purpose becomes reality when we practice His principles. The mission of the Church is empowered when it is filled with vibrant, dedicated faithful stewards.

WHAT DOES DIVINE OWNERSHIP LOOK LIKE?

Have you ever spent time with someone in a public setting who seems to know every person that comes along? The remarkable part is not that they remember more names than humanly possible, it is that they really do *know* the people that pass by. More than just saying "hello," they connect on a much deeper level. I felt it myself the first time I met James Johnson. He was a six foot plus Texas rancher who served on the board of the church I pastored at the time. We grew to be great friends, and I came to depend on his wisdom and direction regarding church decisions.

James was a college graduate and an entrepreneurial businessman. His wife Nelda was a stylist who owned her own salon. They have indeed been richly blessed with material things, and if anyone could say that it belonged to them because they are the ones who had worked hard for it, the Johnsons could. But you would never hear them say that because they realize that all their blessings are *from* God and *for* God. Because of this, they have an immediate awareness of the needs they encounter and are able to willingly and unselfishly respond with generosity.

You have heard the saying about how some people are willing to "give you the shirt off their back"? That is much more than a saying with this couple. I have personally watched them as they jump into action at a moment's notice when they hear about someone who needs help. It could simply be a question that needs answered, or a ride someone needs because their vehicle is being repaired. At work, on the way to church, or just about any public gathering place you can think of, James and Nelda seem to always be ready to help someone out or fill a need because of their unselfish surrender of everything they have to God. People like the Johnsons believe God put them in this world for a purpose. They know they are conduits of God's blessings, and James would be the first to tell you that it all belongs to God.

Through the years God directed me to another ministry and a couple decades passed with very little interaction with the Johnsons except through social media. But not too long ago, when Kathy and I needed some professional advice, the Johnsons came to mind, so Kathy messaged Nelda, and she responded in seconds! They invited us to spend some time with them and their advice helped us through the situation. We were personal beneficiaries of their kindness and willingness to be generous with their time.

I have heard the Johnsons countless times give God all the credit for their success and affirm that everything they have belongs to Him. They find joy in allowing God to use them to meet needs. It may be paying the way for another student to go to a church camp, singing or playing an instrument, taking a family out for a meal after a service on Sunday, or picking up chairs after a church event. Their home is always open, and their hospitality makes you feel like family. The list of ways they have invested the resources that they manage for God over the years, would not fit in the pages of this book. And they do it all without being asked and without expecting anything in return. James and Nelda Johnson are true examples of how Divine Ownership is supposed to look. The difference they have made in the lives of others for all eternity may never be revealed in this life, but God will one day welcome home His good and faithful servants.

CHAPTER THREE

Relationship — It comes with privileges

So now we can rejoice in our wonderful new relationship with God because our Lord Jesus Christ has made us friends of God.

ROMANS 5:11

The discussion of Divine Ownership in the last chapter has no doubt raised the stress level for a lot of readers. Frankly, it's hard for some to imagine how they will get by if they start giving from an already maxed out budget. Most people have more days than dollars left at the end of the month, and trust me, I get that. So, I am asking you to hit the pause button before you panic. This chapter on your relationship with Christ will help you understand how that relationship gives you a firm standing with God that comes with extraordinary blessings. Because of your relationship with Jesus, you no longer just *know* about Him, He lives within you and that gives you an opportunity to reset the way you see things. As you get to know God more intimately you will find that the way you see stuff is changing. Instead of asking, "How can I possibly become a giver?" You will begin to wonder, "How can I possibly *not* become one?"

How we manage resources in the material world has everything to do with our relationship with Christ and will greatly impact our attitude about how we live and give. Spiritual maturity helps us understand that giving is not a "how much do I have to give" issue, but a heartfelt desire to be generous. Over time because of your relationship with Jesus, you will find your attitude evolves from a "got to give" to a "get to give," view. This transformation allows followers of Christ the opportunity to experience worshipful giving in a deep and meaningful way and understand how their obedience in giving is a vital part of their relationship with God.

Rather than dwelling on the issue of how you will become the giver that God intends you to be, let's first set our thoughts on some of the privileges that come to us because of our relationship with Him. Because of Christ, your sins have been forgiven, you have eternal life in heaven, the Holy Spirit now lives within you, and you are *a friend of God*, surrounded by His love. These blessings are just the beginning of the many other privileges that you have perhaps never even considered. As the verse from Romans 5:2 declares, *Because of our faith, Christ has brought us into this place of undeserved privilege where we now stand, and we confidently and joyfully look forward to sharing God's glory.* God fully intends for you to share in His glory. So, let's begin to contemplate what that means. Let's start thinking about how your relationship with God opens the door for you to experience the many blessings that come your way as an obedient child of God. Each of the relational privileges that we discuss adds immense quality and meaning to your life. They cannot be purchased online or at any box store. They are priceless, and freely offered to you as a totally surrendered child of God.

THE PRIVILEGE OF VALUE

Look at the birds. They don't plant or harvest or store food in barns, for your heavenly Father feeds them. And aren't you far more valuable to him than they are?

MATTHEW 6:26

Jesus used the visual image of birds to help His followers understand how important they were to Him. He pointed out that the birds did nothing to earn their food, and yet it was provided for them. I love how Jesus put a question to His

65

listeners that had such an obvious answer. *Aren't you far more valuable* than the birds? I urge you to open your heart to this same question and fully grasp the point Jesus was making. You are valuable in the eyes of Christ. When we grasp how much God values and loves us, we begin to set aside all self-doubt. Recognizing how He sees us, pushes us to rethink how we see ourselves, allowing us to understand the importance of our relationship with Him and what a privilege it is that God provides for us.

Because we live in a world that will use you then lose you, it is sometimes hard to buy into the idea that you are valued with an everlasting love. There is nothing you can do that will ever make God love you any less. Yes, the things we do, good or bad, impact our fellowship with God, but that bond we have with Him, that relationship through Jesus, is unshakable. *And I am convinced that nothing can ever separate us from God's love. Neither death nor life, neither angels nor demons, neither our fears for today nor our worries about tomorrow—not even the powers of hell can separate us from God's love. No power in the sky above or in the earth below—indeed, nothing in all creation will ever be able to separate us from the love of God that is revealed in Christ Jesus our Lord* (Rom. 8:38-39).

So, please don't throw God into the same boat with all those who have betrayed, abandoned, or hurt you in the past.

God is very different. He can be trusted to keep His word and He will always value you as His beloved child. Even before we were born, before we could have done anything to earn God's favor, Romans 5:8, says, *But God showed his great love for us by sending Christ to die for us while we were still sinners.* This kind of love is incomprehensible intellectually and emotionally. It can only be understood by faith. The value God places on us clearly shows what a priceless privilege it is to relationally be part of His family.

THE PRIVILEGE OF PRAYER

So, if you sinful people know how to give good gifts to your children, how much more will your heavenly Father give good gifts to those who ask him.

MATTHEW 7:11

This verse about prayer starts by using the relationship between parents and their children to help us understand how deeply God is committed to us. Because believers are a part of the family of God they are granted the privilege of making requests before their Heavenly Father. We can go directly and boldly to the throne of God (Heb. 4:16) with our fears, our worries, our thanks, and our needs. Our Father in heaven has no equal. He is always good and loving and always desires to give gifts to His children when they live within the safety of

His favor. This privilege of prayer is based on the premise that we are to ask according to His will. *Now this is the confidence that we have in Him, that if we ask anything according to His will, He hears us* (1 John 5:14).

The best way to grow your relationship with God is to know Him better. Like having a new friend, the more time you spend with that person, the more you know their likes and dislikes. So, by spending time with God in His Word and speaking to Him in prayer, you become more familiar with His plans and His heart. As your relationship with God grows, you gain deeper insights into His will for your life. This really comes into play when you manage resources by scriptural principles. Knowing the heart of God and understanding what He sees as valuable then becomes your passionate pursuit.

THE PRIVILEGE OF WORSHIP

Let us come to him with thanksgiving. Let us sing psalms of praise to him. Come, let us worship and bow down. Let us kneel before the Lord our maker, for he is our God. We are the people he watches over, the flock under his care.

PSALM 95:2, 6-7

All around the world, countless Christians from various cultures, nationalities, and languages gather together and worship God. There is only one thing that opens the door for this privilege of worship – our relationship with God through Jesus Christ. Worship is one of the most fundamental relational interactions God's children have with their Heavenly Father. It is an opportunity to love God back through voices of praise. Yet, ironically, we sometimes take this privilege for granted, failing to avail ourselves of joining together with other believers and praising God in Christian community. Equally sad are the times we fail to exercise this privilege on a personal level, by not devoting quiet time to worship Him in our hearts. It is clear that a neglect of worship both in community and in private goes hand in hand with a shallow relationship with God, which then results in an unwillingness to surrender your time and resources.

THE PRIVILEGE OF SPREADING THE GOOD NEWS ABOUT JESUS CHRIST

By God's grace and mighty power, I have been given the privilege of serving him by spreading this Good News.

EPHESIANS 3:7

Paul knew that the people who gladly received the message of hope through Jesus would be changed forever, and it was his privilege to be part of that. We who have a relationship with Jesus are also blessed with the same privilege, both individually and by joining hands with others in cooperative efforts to spread the Gospel. As stewards of God's resources, we should be consumed with the idea of both "giving and going" to bring hope to the hopeless.

For some people, the thought of talking to another person about Jesus brings a sense of apprehension and a type of paralytic anxiety that holds them back from doing what they really want to do and what they know is right. Being paralyzed by the fear of someone's negative response to Jesus, can cause us to miss out on one of our greatest privileges. A certain amount of concern is natural and normal but with preparation and God's help, this angst can be overcome. Pray about your fear. Sharing Christ should be a natural conversation, not a packaged script that you have to memorize. Your relationship with God will allow you to share your personal "Jesus story," which can help lead someone to Him.

One final thought on that subject is that most churches have learning opportunities that teach you how to effectively point the spiritually unresolved to Jesus. They can provide accountability and support for you to develop the confidence you need. The more you tell others what Jesus means to you, the more you will grow in confidence and seize this privilege of sharing the Good News with others.

THE PRIVILEGE OF GIVING

*They begged us again and again for the privilege of sharing
in the gift for the believers in Jerusalem.*

2 CORINTHIANS 8:4

Possibly you have never considered it before, but as the verse says, giving is a privilege. While spreading the Gospel in Macedonia, Paul shared how the church in Jerusalem faced oppression and famine. Because of the relationship they had with Jesus, the church in Corinth, living in poverty and persecution themselves, was moved to give *not only what they could afford, but far more* (2 Cor. 8:3). Today, our world has many places where the political and religious persecution of Christ followers is practiced daily, so now we too like the Corinthians have the special privilege of giving to help the suffering Church both in our own communities and around the world. Caring enough to open our hearts prompts us also to open our wallets; and giving generously to help brothers and sisters in Christ brings a deep sense of joy and reward, knowing we have helped hurting people.

In addition to the religious and political persecution of our brothers and sisters there are natural disasters that leave people homeless and hungry. Earthquakes, hurricanes, drought, and disease, all place immeasurable hardships on Christians and on those who don't yet know Jesus, leaving

71

them powerless to help themselves. That was the case on August 24, 1992, when Hurricane Andrew crashed into the southern tip of Florida with sustained winds of 165 miles an hour, leaving a path of devastation. Forty-four people lost their lives, 82,000 businesses and over 150,000 homes were destroyed. The hurricane caused 25 billion dollars in damages, and now 30 years later is still considered one of the top five hurricanes to strike the U.S.[1] Of course, the Red Cross, the military, and many other organizations came to the rescue, but the disaster also created an opportunity for Christians to shine their light. The church I pastored at the time quickly gathered food, water, and building supplies. We loaded up vans and headed south to make a difference.

Pulling into the lot of what was left of a local church in Homestead, I noticed a work crew already on the church's roof repairing the storm damage. The morning light was just revealing the total devastation of the storm when I realized the vehicles of this crew had North Carolina license plates. Out of curiosity I asked one of them how they had arrived so quickly from so far away. One man shared how eight years ago Hurricane Diana had ripped through the Cape Fear, area of North Carolina and their church had been flooded and nearly destroyed. He said a group of believers from South Florida, had arrived on their property and made repairs immediately, having brought their own supplies with them. I remember him saying, "How could we not show up after that?"

Without even leaving their names these strangers from North Carolina, extended a loving hand of Christian friendship to their hurting brothers and sisters. As they headed to their vehicles, they hugged a few people and told them they would be praying for them and drove away. Their relationship with God had fueled their passion to give of their time and resources to meet the needs of others whom they had never even met before. Jesus was the tie that bound these people from North Carolina to a group of strangers in South Florida. They were connected together in Christ and the givers on this day knew that it was *more blessed to give than to receive* (Acts 20:35). It had been their privilege to be a part of God's answer to the prayers of their hurting fellow believers.

Because giving is both a command and a sacred privilege, it is essential for Christians to accept the immense responsibility of guiding their giving with sound biblical principles that are essential when it comes to developing successful financial management practices. Peter Grandich, author of *Confessions of a Wall Street Whiz Kid,* stated "I get my financial guidance from the Bible." In a recent interview, writer Sheryle Nance-Nash included the following quote about money and the Bible from Grandich: "Our whole culture now is built on the premise that we have to have more money and more stuff to feel happy and secure. Public storage is the poster child for what's wrong with America. We have too much stuff because we've bought into the myth fabricated by Wall Street and Madison Avenue that more stuff equals more happiness. That's the total opposite of the truth, and the opposite of what it says in The Bible."[2] When Grandich was then asked what the number one most important biblical rule of finance was, he answered, "God owns everything."[3] I couldn't have said it better myself!

God expects us to be wise stewards, to make sure we are following scriptural blueprints and investing God's money wisely. Sadly, hucksters and financial con artists do their evil and deceptive work at every turn and often target Christians. It's up to us to vet the recipients of the blessing and responsibility we have to give. So, here are five principles to guide you as you exercise this privilege.

GIVING PRINCIPLE #1:
HOW LITTLE YOU HAVE DOES NOT STOP YOU FROM BEING A GIVER

Now I want you to know, dear brothers and sisters, what God in his kindness has done through the churches in Macedonia. They are being tested by many troubles, and they are very poor. But they are also filled with abundant joy, which has overflowed in rich generosity. For I can testify that they gave not only what they could afford, but far more. And they did it of their own free will.

2 CORINTHIANS 8:1-3

Macedonia is an area that is now known as the south-central Balkans in northern Greece, southwestern Bulgaria, and the Independent Republic of North Macedonia. The churches in this region were used two thousand years ago as an example of generous giving. You can see in the passage that these early followers of Jesus were very poor, and yet they still participated in giving to help those who were going through the great drought and famine that had struck the region around Jerusalem. They believed it was their privilege to share in the gift that was given because it provided some relief for those under severe hardship.

When writing the epistle to the church in Corinth, Paul inspired them to take part in this giving effort. Another underlying lesson found within this giving of a special offering, is that Paul knew the importance of unity in the body of Christ, and how giving would help break down some long-held prejudices that existed between Jewish believers in the church in Jerusalem, and the Gentile believers Paul was ministering to in Macedonia. When he mentioned the faithfulness of the churches in Macedonia, he stressed how they were filled with joy to be a part of this offering of generosity. Paul was careful to tell the church at Corinth that these churches had given from their poverty. He stressed this because he knew that it is just normal and even understandable for someone, who is themselves living in poverty, to feel unable to give to help someone else.

Anyone can be a giver, because helping or serving others isn't just for people with lots of money in their bank accounts. You don't have to give millions to charity to be of service to someone else. Volunteering to visit the aging in a nursing home, or donating unused clothes and household items, or even being a good listener to someone costs nothing but goes a long way in uplifting another person.

GIVING PRINCIPLE #2:
WITH ABUNDANCE COMES ADDED RESPONSIBILITY

> *When someone has been given much, much will be required in return; and when someone has been entrusted with much, even more will be required.*
>
> LUKE 12:48

This principle of added responsibility helps us understand that God does not bless us so that we can consume more personally, but so we can be more of a blessing to others. When God gives us more of His stuff to care for, we are required in return to honor the trust He has placed in us.

Failure to do so, would be a betrayal of His trust. Someone reading this section may wonder why God does not give them more because after all, they believe they are trustworthy enough to manage more resources. I'm not saying that someone with fewer resources is less trustworthy. This issue is more complicated than that. No one can fully know the long-range plans God has regarding why one person lives with abundance and another lives in poverty. The only thing we know for sure is that God is sovereign and all wise. We also know that God uses the absence of wealth to teach us many different spiritual lessons. One thing is absolutely certain, those who are blessed with this world's goods should never forget that those blessings come with a requirement to give more. God is expecting them to wisely manage their material possessions and show God's love through their generosity.

When you have fully embraced the truth of Divine Ownership, you can clearly see the spiritual value of giving generously to needs that are important to God. A willing generosity, a happy giver, emerges as you see first-hand how God uses your giving to impact the lives of those with material and spiritual needs. You demonstrate God's love and presence and allow people to know that God loves them. You begin to see your giving as a privilege, not a burden to bear. This principle of added responsibility for those who have a surplus is not to be taken lightly.

GIVING PRINCIPLE #3:
PRIORITIZE THE WHEN AND WHERE OF GIVING

> *On the first day of each week, you should each put aside a portion of the money you have earned. Don't wait until I get there and then try to collect it all at once.*

1 CORINTHIANS 16:2

Once again writing to the Corinthian church, Paul clearly helps us understand that our local faith community should be the first focus of our giving. He then instructs them to be systematic in their giving, specifying that the first day of the week, Sunday, is when giving should happen. Obviously, those who receive income monthly or even bi-weekly will not be able to give every Sunday. But when the first Sunday rolls around after having received compensation for our efforts, we are instructed to give. Paul also reinforces the principle of proportionality when he says, *a portion of the money you have earned*, should be given on Sunday. We will talk some more about this when we look at Principle #5.

Choosing to make your local church the primary focus of your giving not only follows scriptural examples, but it just makes sense. Giving to your local church ensures accountability that your giving is being used for effective ministry. The leaders in your own local church are able to provide a firsthand accounting of how God's money, given by you, is being invested. There is no greater place to invest God's resources than through the local church where you are a committed member of the body.

After prioritizing your giving through the local church, you have the ability to follow God's leading by giving to ministries beyond the geography of your own community. If you have become burdened for a ministry outside your church, you might be surprised that the church you belong to is already supporting the same burden. Be sure to check with a leader in your church to see if that is the case. You also need to be aware of local church networking practices because sometimes churches band together with other churches and combine collective resources to accomplish an effort or project that would be beyond their individual ability to achieve. This networking uses the wisdom, experience, and knowledge of proven leaders and gives an added layer of accountability allowing generous hearts to give with confidence.

GIVING PRINCIPLE #4:
GIVE CHEERFULLY

> *You must each decide in your heart how much to give. And don't give reluctantly or in response to pressure. For God loves a person who gives cheerfully.*
>
> 2 CORINTHIANS 9:7

Most would agree that in today's economy it can sometimes be difficult to give with the cheerful attitude that Paul was talking about in that passage. Sometimes it's necessary to seek God's guidance to help sort through the thundering sounds of appeals and requests for help that come from every direction. No one person or family can possibly give enough to meet every need, so it's important to consider the urgency of needs as well as our personal abilities to give.

Our giving attitudes are enhanced when we consider the example of Jesus. He is the supreme example of a cheerful giver who willingly left the riches of heaven to come to earth for us. (See Philippians chapter two) When our Lord's sacrifice was so great, might we not also be happy to sacrifice for His purposes? Indeed, everything we have is from Him: *Every good and perfect gift is from above, coming down from the Father of the heavenly lights* (James 1:17).

By giving cheerfully, we display God's glorious grace in our lives. Every time we give for kingdom work, we experience grace and joy, something we should never trade for all the riches in the world. It's important to note that Paul also urged his readers to be generous in giving by using the illustration of a farmer. He said, *a farmer who only plants a few seeds will get a small crop, but the one who plants generously will have a generous crop* (2 Cor. 9:6).

Giving is also a reflection of the heart condition, so if you can't give cheerfully, it means that you and God have some talking to do. He would never want you to give with doubt or if you feel forced in any way. That attitude in giving only breeds bitterness and resentment. Our gifts to God and His kingdom must flow from a heart that is fully in love with the Savior.

GIVING PRINCIPLE #5: PROPORTIONAL GIVING

> *One-tenth of the produce of the land, whether grain from the fields or fruit from the trees, belongs to the Lord and must be set apart to him as holy.*
>
> LEVITICUS 27:30

Just as it is impossible to understand trigonometry without first having a foundation of basic addition, subtraction, multiplication, and division, so it is impossible to understand proportional giving before you have grown a foundational relationship with Jesus. With this thought in mind, don't be so hard on yourself if you are having a hard time with the "mathematics" of faith giving. It can be difficult to fully grasp until your faith has grown, so the remainder of this chapter is to help you take your next step of spiritual growth and be ready to experience proportional giving.

Let's start with something basic. Not everyone's monthly bank statement shows the same amount of money being deposited each month. The amount of surplus one person has when the month ends is sometimes greater than the entirety of another person's income. This financial reality would leave many incapable of giving if everyone in the church was required to give the same amount. God in His wisdom has designed proportional giving so that everyone can participate. As managers of God's possessions our faithfulness is not determined by how much we give but by this standard of proportional giving.

So, what is the basis for the proportional amount? In the Old Testament, God set this proportional standard of giving for His children at ten percent. These standards or laws were intended not only to remind them that everything they had belonged to the Lord, but it was also a way for them to give back to God and thank Him for what they had received. The ten percent requirement meant that everyone could participate. If someone harvested more in their agricultural setting, their ten percent offering would be higher than someone who harvested less. Likewise, ten percent of nothing earned, meant that nothing was required, but the ten percent standard remained the same. By the time we reach the last book in the Old Testament, the people had stopped giving, so the prophet Malachi was inspired by God to write these words:

Should people cheat God? Yet you have cheated me! But you ask, 'What do you mean? When did we ever cheat you?' You have cheated me of the tithes and offerings due to me. You are under a curse, for your whole nation has been cheating me. Bring all the tithes into the storehouse so there will be enough food in my Temple. If you do, says the Lord of Heaven's Armies, I will open the windows of heaven for you. I will pour out a blessing so great you won't have enough room to take it in! Try it! Put me to the test! (Mal. 3:8-10).

This ten percent, or tithe, was not just a random number. Even before the Old Testament law was put in place by Moses, this proportional standard had already been practiced by others who worshiped God. Going back a thousand years before Moses, a tithe or ten percent was given by Abraham to a man of God named Melchizedek (Gen. 14:20). Abraham gave a tithe to him as a gift to God. In the New Testament

(Hebrews chapter 7), we see that Melchizedek was a priest, outside of the Levitical order established by the law of Moses, just as Jesus was, so this tithe standard had credibility and precedent. Still, there are those who believe that the proportionate standard, or tithe, is relevant only to the Old Testament. But Jesus confirmed the tithe as the standard during His ministry on earth in Matthew 23:23, when He scorned the Pharisees saying, *Hypocrites! For you are careful to tithe even the tiniest income from your herb garden, but you ignore the more important aspects of the law – justice, mercy, and faith. You should tithe, yes, but do not neglect the more important things.*

In that passage, Jesus confirmed the tithe, but He also wanted them to continue displaying other godly qualities. Divine Ownership is such a big deal that Jesus spent a large part of his brief three-and-a-half years of earthly ministry stressing the importance of being faithful stewards. He taught about ownership and the role of a steward on many occasions, often using a parable to bring clarity to this profound principle (such as the Parable of the Faithful Servant in Matthew 24).

Jesus's affirmation should remove any doubt that tithing remains the standard even during this present age. Jesus was also much more concerned with how and why we give, more than how much is given. He continually rebuked the wrong kind of giving that was done for show, and pressed people to surrender their hearts completely as well as their resources. Tithing is not a legalistic obligation for Christians today. In fact, most of the New Testament examples of giving go far beyond a ten percent tithe. The tithe serves as a starting place, a principle to guide us because it is equitable and fair. It also remains a way to show our love for God, to acknowledge that He owns everything, and to express our gratitude for the gift of God's grace through Jesus Christ.

Giving proportionally allows the giver to manage the remaining ninety percent and trust that God can make it go further than the full one hundred percent. This kind of faith relies on the goodness of God and encourages followers of Jesus to give out of love not out of duty and obligation. The law made tithing a requirement, but grace calls for a response to the blessings, provisions, and privileges we experience from God's hand. If we believe God to be good, then we also have to believe that the standard of a tithe is for our good as well as for the good of advancing His purposes on earth.

Anyone who concludes that they can't afford to do something as simple as giving ten percent of their income to God has already missed the point. God does not need your money, but He does want all of your heart. The value of putting God first and giving Him the first ten percent of all you acquire demonstrates your surrender and your faith. Now keep this in mind, your relationship with God is not just about giving money. The truth is, you can systematically give a tithe without having fully surrendered everything to God, but you cannot be fully surrendered to God if you are not willing to put Him first in your giving. Tithing is a giant leap of faith and as scripture plainly says, you will never please God if you refuse to exercise faith and trust Him enough to be a giver. *But without faith it is impossible to please Him, for he who comes to God must believe that He is, and that He is a rewarder of those who diligently seek Him* (Heb. 11:6).

The privileges we have because of our relationship with Jesus open up previously unthinkable opportunities. I urge you to fully embrace how much you are loved and valued by God; to experience the privileges of worship and prayer; to see yourself and the world through God's eyes, and let those blessings and privileges prepare you to see and participate in the grace of giving.

WHAT DOES A RELATIONSHIP WITH JESUS FILLED WITH PRIVILEGE LOOK LIKE?

Ted Elliot was raised in a strict religious home in the 1960's. He went to church twice on Sunday and even attended the Wednesday night Bible study, but oddly enough, he never understood the Gospel. In fact, he hardly ever knew much about Jesus at all, because the message he heard over and over was about an angry God in the Old Testament. By the time he was 14 years old, he had determined that the Church was full of hypocrites and that everyone was going to hell. So, he walked away from God and the Church, figuring that if he was going to hell, he may as well have fun along the way. And he did.

As a young man of 19, he met and married his wife Mary who had also been raised with a strict religious background. From there, Ted went to work with an international hotel chain and soon became a rising star within the company. By the time he was 25, he was managing a 750-seat night club, an environment inundated with drugs, promiscuity, and alcohol. Murders on-site and other lude activities were a normal part of life in this particular hotel location.

All this, combined with anger issues from his childhood, created a bad situation for the family, and as their children started coming along, the Elliot's decided that something needed to change. Ted quit his job and the family moved North, hoping for a fresh start. Their daughter was enrolled in a Christian school that required the family to attend church. So, they did.

The first time they walked through the church doors, Mary felt an "awakening" inside her. The pastor preached about the love of Jesus, something neither of them had ever heard or understood before. In order to learn more, Mary invited the pastor and one of the deacons to their home for lunch. When the issue of church membership came up, Ted responded that the church is just full of hypocrites, to which the deacon replied, "Yes, and we have room for two more."

That deacon's honest reply came from that privilege of honest evaluation. He was able to see himself and others the way God sees, and it stirred something in the hearts of the Elliot's. They turned to Jesus, and everything changed. They began to see how that even in their sinful state, the hand of God had always been there guiding, directing them back to Him. As Ted says, "God has a velvet glove on one hand, and a 2x4 in the other." And though he admittedly usually went with the 2x4, Ted knows now that it's the only way he survived those early years.

The Elliott's would tell you that living outside of God's privilege is like being in a never-ending rainstorm without an umbrella. You constantly get wet. They would tell you that it is far better to get out of the storm and go away from the consequences of sin. It isn't that all the storms of life suddenly went away for the Elliot's, but now, as children of God, they were privileged to experience His forgiveness, protection, and provision. Ted eventually became the CEO of a major company in South Florida, where their family became members of the church I pastored there.

As is always the case, when a home embraces God's gifts, blessings followed. Ted and Mary's hearts were now aligned with God's heart and so were their priorities. Resources were now directed toward areas that mattered to their Heavenly Father and they did much more than just give money, they gave themselves to the mission of the Church. Their natural gifts in music were now directed toward leading worship, and the instruments they played brought praise to the Giver of their salvation and spiritual privilege.

Over the years I have watched Ted and Mary continue in their journey of faith. The gifts of discernment and wisdom that they were privileged to receive from God's Word guide them in their living and giving. Because of where they have been they know with absolute certainty what a privilege it is to steward their lives and resources for God's work on this earth and have found that each new day brings exciting new opportunities.

CHAPTER FOUR

Trust – It must be grown

Trust in the Lord with all your heart; do not depend on your own understanding. Seek his will in all you do, and he will show you which path to take.

PROVERBS 3:5-6

When I was 19, I met the girl of my dreams. She was singing on stage at a youth rally. She had beautiful long red hair and the voice of an angel. I knew at that moment that one day I would marry that girl. And I did. What I didn't know, however, was how we would grow to trust God together.

Kathy and I came from similar backgrounds. We were both born in Ohio, we both had stay-at-home moms, and we were both raised in a church-going family, so we learned about God when we were young. Kathy's dad had dropped out of high school to work on the family farm, and my dad had quit school and joined the Navy. Both our dads worked blue-collar jobs that provided for the family's needs, but there was never really much thought about sending kids to college, so as it turns out, we were both the first in our families to earn college degrees.

We met while students and married young. As newlyweds we were on our own. We took no student loans and had no financial support from our parents (who couldn't have given us a dime if they'd wanted to), so we both worked full time jobs and paid the college one month at a time barely staying ahead of our financial obligation. In addition to working, we carried full class schedules, volunteered at our church, and also traveled with the college's ministry teams that connected with high school students around the country.

Kathy had always been involved with the music programs in her school and church and began singing solos at an early age. When she was 16 years old, a member of her home church recognized her vocal gifts and financed an LP album of Christian music. (For those of you who don't know, that's a long-playing vinyl record.) She was occasionally asked to be the featured vocalist for mission trips or to sing for various churches in the area, something that continued even after we were married.

On one such occasion, a small church with a congregation of less than 50 invited Kathy to sing for a special Sunday evening event. We sold three of her albums that night for a grand total of nine dollars. What a blessing! We left that church service and hurried to the local grocery store because after paying the rent, utilities, and college bill, we didn't have any funds left for groceries. Aside from half a box of oatmeal, there was nothing much left in the pantry, and we were a bit on the hungry side. But even though the cost of groceries in the 70's was much less than they are now, we knew that nine dollars wouldn't go far. I know this sounds bizarre to some of you because these days a specialty coffee drink could cost as much.

Kathy and I had already decided from the beginning of our life together that everything we had belonged to God, and we determined to give back to Him at least ten percent of what we earned. That meant that we owed God ninety cents from the cash that was at the moment burning a hole in our pockets. Nine dollars wasn't a lot, but it was the only thing standing between an empty cupboard and our next paychecks.

Standing beside the grocery buggy I remembered our promise to give a tithe back to God, but the problem was, we had already spent God's part of the money. So, together we surveyed the buggy and selected the necessary items to put back on the shelf and resolved to put the recovered ninety cents in the offering at church the next Sunday. Aside from the fact that we didn't go hungry, the lesson we learned is that God is trustworthy and through the nearly fifty years of our marriage we have continued to faithfully give to God and His purposes. And guess what – our pantry has never been empty. The lesson for us was clear, God could be trusted. For us, this leap of faith was a defining moment.

In the process of learning to trust God with everything, Kathy and I didn't run to that commitment like an Olympic sprinter crossing the finish line. In all honestly, we were probably more like Frodo who struggled to surrender the ring. Our possessions – all our stuff – can be a powerful force and letting go is challenging. But we are so thankful we came to the right decision and have fully trusted God ever since.

Intellectually buying into Divine Ownership is the easy part while putting it into practice is another matter. But once you resolve in your heart to be a giver and not a taker, you will experience that defining moment as we did. Like Joshua you can say, *As for me and my family we will serve the Lord* (Josh. 24:15).

We have such an amazing God. There is absolutely nothing that happens in our vast universe that is beyond His power and authority. God has the right to exercise His power over all things. He not only holds the entire universe in the palm of His hands, but He cares for and guides each of us individually. He gives us our breath and even controls our destiny (Dan. 5:23). God can be trusted. Knowing that He is good is the foundation of trust.

The more we trust God, the more our faith grows, not just in the easy times, but the hard times as well. Christians who fully trust the Lord through the valleys of life believe deeply that God is always aware of their challenges, yet they still joyfully hold onto His goodness and continue trusting. Corrie Ten Boom who survived the horrible atrocities of the Holocaust said, "Never be afraid to trust the unknown future to a known God."[1] She would certainly know.

There are some, however, who don't trust God completely because their confidence in God's sufficiency in all things has not been personally established. They haven't seen Him provide for them at that last moment like Abraham did. They haven't seen God turn a bad situation into something wonderful like Joseph did, and they haven't wept at a second chance like Peter did. So, they naturally struggle trusting God, especially in the area of their finances. That is why in the previous chapter we learned how the privileges of a close relationship with God must be experienced before anyone can truly trust Him enough to surrender to Divine Ownership.

FAITH AND TRUST ARE INSEPARABLE

The words *faith* and *trust* are inseparable in God's vocabulary, and as you read this book, you will notice that the words are even used interchangeably. That is because the ancient Greek word *pistis* which is translated 'faith' is a variation of the word 'trust.' Genuine faith gives evidence of His presence in our lives when it is demonstrated through actions of trust. If we say we have faith in God but do not trust Him to keep His promises and provisions for us, we are either deceiving ourselves or have weak faith that needs to be nurtured and grown. *What good is it, dear brothers and sisters, if you say you have faith but don't show it by your actions? Can that kind of faith save anyone?* (James 2:14)

James is not saying that actions or works save us. That would be inconsistent with the Bible teachings that salvation is a free gift of God's grace. Instead, James is warning against superficial faith. A faith that is not first established in a relationship with Jesus Christ is a false faith and will not produce the actions or behaviors of a true believer. Authentic faith is deeply rooted in a genuine walk with Christ and the proof of its authenticity is in our actions of trust.

Trusting Jesus for our salvation is an event followed by a process. Some would call this process "sanctification" or "growing in Christ," because over time as we receive more spiritual nourishment, our faith and trust grows. Just as a body builder grows stronger by the stress of lifting heavy weights, the weights that burden your "faith muscles" are able to make you spiritually stronger. Weak faith or even a lack of faith is evidence that basic truths from God's Word have not been learned. *You have been believers so long now that you ought to be teaching others. Instead, you need someone to teach you again the basic things about God's word. You are like babies who need milk and cannot eat solid food* (Heb. 5:12).

The story of Jesus walking on the water during a storm on the Sea of Galilee illustrates for us the power of faith. The raging winds and waves provided the perfect backdrop for Jesus to teach His frightened disciples a powerful truth. It was because of the lessons learned during the storm that these disciples were transformed into men of faith as they witnessed the trustworthiness of Jesus.

But Jesus spoke to them at once. "Don't be afraid," he said. Take courage. I am here!" Then Peter called to him, "Lord if it's really you, tell me to come to you, walking on the water." Yes, come," Jesus said. So, Peter went over the side of the boat and walked on the water toward Jesus. But when he saw the strong wind and the waves he was terrified and began to sink. "Save me, Lord!" he shouted. Jesus immediately reached out and grabbed him. "You have so little faith," Jesus said. "Why did you doubt me?"

When they climbed back into the boat, the wind stopped. Then the disciples worshiped him. "You really are the Son of God!" they exclaimed (Matt. 14:27-33).

The storms of life and periods of doubt and fear are unavoidable. Going beneath the surface of a raging sea is not something any of us wishes for but it is something every one of us needs. If we never faced the raging sea, how would we ever know the depth of God's ability to save us? It is during those times we hear the voice of Jesus saying, *Take courage. I am here!* That is when we can put our eyes back on the One who can calm the storms we experience. And, before you get too hard on Peter for taking his eyes off Jesus and focusing on the storm, remember he was the only one who got out of the boat. Like Peter, we too need to get out of the security of our familiar boats and trust Jesus to do the impossible.

Financial challenges are clearly one of the most common and reoccurring storms of life. It is so easy to take your eyes away from Jesus and focus on the lightning and thunder of economic storms. Just remember, you can go to Jesus even when others stay in the boat. Even if you have gotten out of the boat a few times and followed His voice only to take a swim, you can be sure He continues to reach His hand toward yours. Over time (and after multiple near drownings) you finally get it through your heart and head that Jesus will always be there in the storm.

The impossible becomes a comfortable place to be when you see the presence of Jesus all around you. That trust becomes the bedrock foundation of your life, and you realize that you are protected by the promises that can only be experienced under the umbrella of Divine Ownership. This is how David, the shepherd was able to say, *Even when I walk through the darkest valley, I will not be afraid, for you are close beside me* (Psa. 23:4).

THE DANGER OF DOUBT

Doubt is the enemy that seeks to destroy our trust in God. Let's go back once more to the Garden of Eden where Adam and Eve were instructed not to eat from one specific tree. The very first words the serpent spoke to Eve were to cause doubt. Just as he did during the temptation of Jesus in the New Testament, Satan misquoted God's words. *Did God really say you must not eat the fruit from* **any** (emphasis mine) *of the trees in the garden?* (Gen. 3:1). In defense, Eve explains that there is only *one* tree they must not eat from or even touch or they will die. But the serpent who is very skilled at playing mind games, raises more doubt in verse 4, *You will not surely die* (NKJV). Can't you just hear the deception oozing from his tongue? And we know the rest of the story. Adam and Eve failed to trust God, bringing down the entire human race all because of that little, tiny bit of carefully placed doubt.

So, it would appear that the extent of doubt is far reaching. The more a person's trust has been battered, the harder it is ever to trust again, even making that individual skeptical of God. As it pertains to living out the principle of Divine Ownership, those who have grown in their faith have confidence in the Heavenly Father and are able to give without doubt or fear. They know the goodness of God in a personal way and feel privileged to give. They know that God will provide all their needs.

In contrast, doubters of God don't fully believe in His ability to provide for them, they just don't trust Him. Many feel betrayed by God because of what they perceive to be unanswered prayer, feeling that God abandoned them in their hour of need. Mary and Martha were disappointed when Jesus delayed coming to heal their brother Lazarus, but I don't think anyone would argue that raising Lazarus from the dead was a much bigger deal than just healing his sickness (John 11:1-45). Sadly, many walk away from their faith in God before they understand His divine strategy behind what at first seemed like unanswered prayer. Doubt has sabotaged their trust and derailed their relationship with God, often times forever.

Others doubt God because they walk by sight and not by faith. (See 2 Cor. 5:7.) They need to *see* the hand of God before they *believe* His ability. The doubting disciple Thomas refused to believe that Jesus had risen from the grave until he saw the nail prints in His hands. Jesus gave Thomas the proof he was looking for, saying, *You believe because you have seen me. Blessed are those who believe without seeing me* (John 20:29). Can you see how that last verse applies to you and me? When evidence of God's miracle-working ability is required, it is no longer faith, because *faith is the evidence of things **not** seen* (Heb. 11:1, emphasis mine).

Still some people doubt or stop trusting God because they actually fear the unknown. I recently read that "trusting God has consequences."[2] At first, I didn't get it, but the more I thought about it, the more it made perfect sense. Sometimes, completely trusting God and following His direction leads to some pretty scary places, like when someone's heart is pulled toward missionary work in a strange and foreign land, away from family and the comforts of home. God moves us from those comfort zones on purpose. It's the only way we build faith and trust in Him, which is why I believe that trust is a learned behavior as we build more trust upon previous trust.

TRUSTBUSTERS

A trustbuster is anything that draws your faith away from God. Allowing anything or anyone to take God's place can only end in disappointment, because no one can ever be as powerful as our omnipotent God, who is *glorious in power* (Ex. 15:6). He is almighty (Jer. 32:27), and He is a *jealous God* (Ex. 20:5) who is displeased when His children falsely trust another power. In those times, God is the loving Father who works to draw our reliance back to Him.

TRUSTBUSTER #1: TRUSTING IN SELF

> *Those who trust their own insight are foolish, but anyone who walks in wisdom is safe.*
>
> PROVERBS 28:26

Some people prefer to put all their confidence in themselves instead of God. These people have disregarded John the Baptist's teaching that *He must become greater, and I must become less and less* (John 3:30). An example of this is King Saul in 1 Samuel 13 when the Israelites were preparing to face the Philistine's massive army. The prophet Samuel instructed Saul to wait for him in Gilgal and he would come and offer sacrifice to God before the battle. But when Samuel delayed his arrival, Saul took it upon himself to handle things and sacrificed the burnt offering himself. Just at that moment the prophet of God arrived. Saul, of course justified his error and even blamed Samuel for not getting there sooner. Very foolish! Samuel told him, *You have not kept the command the Lord your God gave you…now your kingdom must end* (1 Sam. 13:14). The passage goes on to say that if Saul would have trusted God and followed His commands, God would have established Saul's kingdom over Israel forever, but because of his ego and his "I can do it myself attitude," Saul was rejected.

Egotistical self-reliance over trusting God is never a good thing. But too often, this attitude is the reason some choose not to trust God. They don't believe that God is as able as they are. They would rather put their confidence in themselves. Self-reliance carries over to areas of finance as well. Why should they trust God with their giving when they alone have earned the money? They refuse to believe in God's Divine Ownership, exalting their own abilities above God's.

TRUSTBUSTER #2: TRUSTING IN OTHER PEOPLE

> *There are "friends" who destroy each other, but a real friend sticks closer than a brother.*
>
> **PROVERBS 18:24**

It's been said that the only people who can hurt you or break your heart are the people that you are closest to and trust the most. Lots of people disappoint us from time to time, but the cut of betrayal by someone you had previously held in high regard goes the deepest. (Sheryl Crow would agree.) Such betrayal of trust has ultimately led to the ruin of many relationships, and without God's help empowering you to extend true forgiveness, there is usually little or no possibility of rebuilding trust with that person who betrayed you.

Trusting and depending on other people to provide everything you need is a shaky life plan at best, because far too often people let us down. They may not always mean to, but sometimes it just happens. It's just foolish to believe that another human being can care for you and be dependable to you in the same way that God can and does do.

It's also foolish to think that the *word* of another person can be as trustworthy as God's. Jacob trusted his Uncle Laban's word that he would be able to marry Rachel after working seven years, but Laban deceived him and gave him Leah instead. Laban was untrustworthy and it cost Jacob another seven years of his life. Also, Joseph through no fault of his own, found himself in an Egyptian prison and trusted that his prison mate, the Pharoah's cupbearer, would speak good of him when he was removed from prison. But Genesis

40:23 says the *cupbearer did not remember Joseph.* His word proved untrustworthy.

Not long ago, Kathy and I experienced this truth personally when we sought some advice from a financial "expert." We were concerned about some tax implications, so we asked all the right questions and trusted the financial advisor's answers. Big mistake! We felt betrayed by this person who should have known better, and who of course, took no responsibility for the situation. Kathy and I know that nobody's word is ever as good as God's, so we kept trusting Him to get us through that rough spot. God supplied our every need through the wise council of a Christian CPA who helped us work through the problem. Even when people fail us, God will always provide a way.

So often in the vicious cycle of betrayal, disappointment turns to hurt, hurt turns to anger, anger to bitterness and we find ourselves in a downward spiral like a plane spinning toward the ground. This is when many people put up walls to protect themselves from being hurt again. There is only one path to follow when you discover that your trust in someone else has been misplaced. With God's help you must forgive and then turn your trust back to God. If you are feeling the sting of betrayal and disappointment because someone let you down, please choose forgiveness over festering bitterness, because without even realizing it, you may allow your loss of trust in a person to then impact your trust and relationship in God.

TRUSTBUSTER #3:
TRUSTING IN CIVIL GOVERNMENT

When the godly are in authority, the people rejoice. But when the wicked are in power, they groan.

PROVERBS 29:2

You don't have to listen to the political commentators very long to see this verse in action. There is a lot of groaning going on. Corruption, graft, deception, and hypocrisy run rampant in the stories broadcast about those in authority. As bad as those behaviors are, they are only the symptoms of the real problem. Leaders who do not lead with the absolute truths of God's Word to guide them are doomed to make a mess of things. Then their failures have a trickle-down effect on the people who trusted in the promises of that favored politician, leading to total disillusionment. Their hopes for government to save them are crushed when they discover that their misplaced confidence is on sinking sand, while people who have chosen to put their trust in the Lord know better.

Still, many people choose to look toward civil government for all their provisions. History has taught us with certainty, human government is flawed because it is made up of flawed humans. Without checks and balances that limit the corrupt Adamic nature found in everyone, all civil governments will crumble from within. The further a nation is from God the more corrupt it will become and the greater the potential is for the trust you place in them to be torn asunder. Civil government will always come short of providing a dependable and trustworthy foundation for your life. This myth of a utopian form of government that takes care of all the needs of all the people all of the time, is a dangerous fairy tale and believing it is naïve.

The good news is that the entire history of the early Church takes place in the midst of a corrupt pagan government that was hostile to Christianity and yet the Church not only survived, but it thrived. If you do not want to be hurt by the false promises of politicians, regardless of their party, understand that you can't just trust them whole-heartedly. Always remember, our trust is in God.

But just to be clear, also remember that even though our trust is in God and not in political leaders, we still have certain responsibilities to government authorities. God's Word is clear on that.

- *Pray for those in authority. Pray this way for kings and all who are in authority so that we can live peaceful and quiet lives marked by godliness and dignity* (1 Tim. 2:2).

- *Pay your taxes to those in authority. Pay your taxes and government fees to those who collect them* (Rom. 13:7).

- *Give respect to those who are in authority, even when it is not deserved. Give respect and honor to those who are in authority* (Rom. 13:7).

TRUSTBUSTER #4: TRUSTING IN AN EMPLOYER

Never take advantage of poor and destitute laborers, whether they are fellow Israelites or foreigners living in your towns.

DEUTERONOMY 24:14

Over the years I have meet countless people who were putting their trust in a job, a career, or a company. They believed that if they worked hard and remained loyal, they would be taken care of by the employer. But when the unexpected pink slip came, it was a bitter pill to swallow.

In the early 20th century, IBM (International Business Machines) was a growing, thriving company. They espoused a "cradle to grave," culture, meaning that if you got in, the company would always be there for you. They hosted regular carnivals and picnics for the employees and their families and even provided numerous country clubs and golf courses all around the country where workers could play for next to nothing. Respect for the employees was a core value and for a long time they could proudly say that in 70 years they had never laid off workers. Job security. Happy workplace. "But then, in 1993, the unthinkable happened: sixty thousand workers lost their jobs. Even for workers who knew the company was in bad shape, it was a tough day."[3]

And who could have foreseen the COVID pandemic of 2020 that totally changed the workforce. "The transformation of our labor markets, the use of technology, the change in our behaviors as consumers, and our shifting expectations of how, where and when we want to work, will have a lasting impact. This will lead to job losses in areas of sales, office and administration support, higher education, air travel and hotels as well as in the construction industry."[4]

You can never forget, the economy and the jobs we work are fragile and untrustworthy deliverers of peace. Even highly principled businesses are subject to world conditions beyond their control, and people lose their livelihood every day, but if it should happen to you, remember God has not failed you. Trusting in a corporation may prove to be a trustbuster, but when faith and trust are firmly anchored in God, we are able to weather any hardship or financial crisis. So, if all your hope is in a job, you will need to shift your trust to the One who can carry you through the most difficult of circumstances.

TRUSTBUSTER #5:
TRUSTING IN RELIGIOUS LEADERS

> *They are blind guides leading the blind, and if one blind person guides another, they will both fall into a ditch.*
>
> MATTHEW 15:14

Let me begin by saying that it is important and reasonable to look up to our spiritual leaders. God has put them in our lives to be examples and to help us grow spiritually. But in the verse from Matthew 15, Jesus is talking about the religious leaders of His day who had lost all credibility and had led others to fall into the same ditch they had dug for themselves. On another occasion Jesus called some of the religious leaders *whitewashed tombs—beautiful on the outside but filled on the inside with dead people's bones* (Matt. 23:27). Jesus reserved His harshest words for those so-called spiritual leaders who made a mockery of their office.

Few things are more devastating than when a religious leader falls short of the ideals of their calling. Although we know that no one should be put on a pedestal and that everyone is capable of falling, all of us are shocked when we hear the latest sordid story of a religious leader who is caught doing something shameful. The crushing disappointment is not easy to get over even for those who have been in church all their lives. For many, even their faith and trust in God is shaken. Satan knows all this, so it's important that you hold up your spiritual pastors and teachers in prayer. They wear a bullseye in the spiritual war and face the enemy at the front line of the battle. If just one leader is brought low, the enemy knows that many will follow. He also knows that your disillusionment in religious leaders will directly affect your wallet and crush your desire to give joyfully.

The answer to restoring your faith and rebuilding trust is the same no matter who or what is the source of that distrust. It's not enough to push the hurt into the back of your mind and "cowboy up." Suppressed hurt will reemerge in very real ways. When someone close to you betrays you, the pain of that betrayal will hold you back from getting close to someone again. When civil government fails you, your trust in authority will waver. When one of your spiritual giants falls, your faith in God could also be devastated. All these trust issues will affect your walk with Christ, your faith in your entire belief system, and even the idea that God owns everything.

GROWING TRUST

We do this by keeping our eyes on Jesus, the champion who initiates and perfects our faith. Because of the joy awaiting him, he endured the cross, disregarding its shame. Now he is seated in the place of honor beside God's throne.

HEBREWS 12:2

An antidote to doubt and distrust is to turn your attention back to Jesus. Because the world is screaming for your attention, it often seems like an overwhelming challenge to stay focused on Him, but it can be done, especially when we follow the words of Hebrews 12:1-2. That passage encourages us to cast off the weight of sin and to run the race with confidence *by keeping our eyes on Jesus, the champion who initiates and perfects our faith.* It's like the classic hymn says, "Turn your eyes upon Jesus. Look full in His wonderful face, and the things of earth will grow strangely dim in the light of His glory and grace."[5]

A daily habit of reading God's Word also strengthens faith and grows trust. The Apostle Paul taught us that *faith comes by hearing, and hearing by the word of God* (Rom. 10:17 NKJV). His Word is the foundation that builds a deep and abiding confidence in His omnipotent ability to do what He has promised. In the Sermon on the Mount, Jesus said, *Anyone who listens to my teachings and follows it is wise, like a*

112

person who builds a house on solid ground. Though the rain comes in torrents and the floodwaters rise and the winds beat against that house, it won't collapse because it is built on bedrock. But anyone who hears my teaching and doesn't obey it is foolish, like a person who builds a house on sand (Matt. 7:24-26).

Metaphorically, the rain, the floods, and the wind in that passage are those challenges and hardships that lead to doubt that potentially takes our eyes off God; but standing firm in the truth and power of His Word provides resilience as well as fertile soil to grow even greater trust in Him. I encourage you to follow His teachings and trust His Holy Word to be the light to guide your path (Psa.119:105), because His Word, and only His Word is trustworthy, infallible, and will never let you down.

Our faith is also strengthened when we spend time in sweet communication with God. Nineteenth century author and attorney, E.M. Bounds wrote many books on the subject of prayer. He said, "Trust perfected is prayer perfected."[6] I believe that. There is a direct correlation between the depth of our trust in God and the amount of time we spend communicating with Him. Likewise, In the book *The Hour that Changes the World*, author Dick Eastman tells us, "Where there is an absence of prayer, there is an absence of power."[7]

No wonder the Bible tells us to *pray without ceasing* (1 Thess. 5:17).

There are some people though who instead of personally listening to the Spirit's voice in quiet times of prayer, prefer to let someone else do the listening and assume they can just benefit from that person's experience. "Let them tell us what God is saying, after all, isn't that why we pay preachers?"[8] But that kind of indirect relationship with God won't ever build trust.

Becoming a part of a faith community is another way to build your faith. Surrounding yourself with other believers can encourage you along the way. *Two are better than one…if either of them falls down, one can help the other up. But pity anyone who falls and has no one to help them up* (Eccl. 4:9-10 NIV).

I think it's safe to say that everyone has some degree of trust issues. But don't let small seeds of doubt disrupt growing a solid relationship with God. When doubt creeps in, focus on the Savior and listen to the assuring voice of the Holy Spirit within which requires some one-on-one time with God. Learn to listen to His voice. As John 12:27 says, *My sheep hear my voice; I know them, and they follow me.* Trust God, tune your ear to listen for His voice and follow Him.

TRUST AND THE SCHOOL OF HARD KNOCKS

Over the years I have counselled countless people about the challenges of trusting God. They almost always want to know why it's so hard to let go of the stuff and let God take control. I always tell them that if it were easy, if we never knew what it was to be in need, we would never know what it is to depend on God. We would never understand His miraculous ability. Sometimes it is necessary for God to lead us to those places of desperation; a place where we have nowhere else to turn except to Him. This is a hard truth, but trusting God requires us to reject the idea that we are completely self-sufficient.

Heartbreak, disappointment, and economic hard knocks are harsh teachers, but their lessons are not soon forgotten. You just can't learn life-altering trust any other way than going through the discomfort and stress that comes from having earnestly asked God to carry you through your problem. As the Bible teaches *We can rejoice, too, when we run into problems and trials, for we know that they help us develop endurance. And endurance develops strength of character, and character strengthens our confident hope of salvation. And this hope will not lead to disappointment* (Rom. 5:3-5). Indeed, it is in the school of hard knocks that we learn beyond a shadow of doubt that God can be trusted to meet our every financial need and even dig us out of a hole that is perhaps a result of your own folly.

As mentioned before, one of the great privileges of being a Christian is that we can hold everything up to the light of scripture and see the world from God's perspective. His Word lights the path we are to follow and guides us in making wise decisions. We can practice Divine Ownership, free of doubt and fully trust in God rather than in other people or other things. Yes, there will still be momentary disappointments when individuals or institutions fail us, but our spiritual, emotional, intellectual, and even financial needs are secure in the trust we place in God. *God's way is perfect. All the Lord's promises prove true* (Psa. 18:30).

This chapter has been intended to help you see the connection between trusting God and affirming Divine Ownership and becoming a faithful steward of His possessions. Trusting Jesus for your salvation is only pie in the sky if you do not trust Him enough to surrender control of the resources that your Savior has given you to manage.

If you believe in your heart that you fully trust Jesus, look a little deeper and assess the way you manage your finances. Is God directing the way you plan your budget? Are you a giver? The issue of giving is one of the strongest indicators that will reveal whether you fully trust God or not. When someone says, "I can't understand how I will make it if I return a percentage of my income back to God," they are questioning whether God can be trusted. This lack of faith in God forces you to seek other things to trust. As we have already discussed those other trust options fail, and the result of that false trust is always a troubled heart, fear, depression, and lack of peace.

WHAT DOES TRUST LOOK LIKE?

Another lay-off, another long drive home that was filled with a gut wrenching dread at the thought of telling the family yet again, that the company that claimed it could be trusted by their loyal employees could in fact, *not* be. This moment was both the end and the beginning. It was now crystal clear; no longer would he put his faith in a company to provide for the needs of his family. Moving forward Tom's life would be all about fully trusting in God and God alone.

For years, Tom had been a loyal employee of one of the top retail stores in the country, hired as their appliance repair man. Even prior to his employment there, Tom had done this type of work, but once employed by the company was made to sign a non-compete clause. This was not a problem until the company started lay-offs, which then prohibited him from providing for his family even from that previous line of work. Though he had skills and a work ethic, his hands were tied legally. His family of four would go for periods of time with little to no income.

Not long after, rumors began circulating that the retail chain would be closing their doors permanently. Tom realized that something had to change. He walked into a Subway shop that day and an idea came to him. How would it be to own a franchise? What would be involved? He called his sister to ask her advice only to discover that she had the exact same idea at the exact same time. They began to pray about the possibility.

Tom's prayer was that if this endeavor would harm his family in any way that God would close the doors. But the doors never closed. One day while walking around his property, he saw a crumpled up piece of trash, and when he picked it up discovered that it was a Subway wrapper. Tom took it as a sign, and he and his sister proceeded with their plan, trusting God all the way.

The entire family was involved. Tom's wife, Ruth, became the manager of the shop, working long hours to get the business off the ground, and their sons, James and John, became the store's first sandwich artists. Tom, who was now able to also continue his appliance repair business, worked both jobs to keep the family going. But long hours, hard work and a high standard of excellence soon made their first investment profitable. They reinvested the gains they made from the first restaurant into another and then followed the same formula again. Through it all they remained faithful to God in their tithes and offerings and God continued to bless in return. Today Tom and his sister own seven Subway shops and are praying about adding another next year. Their family's trust in God was well founded.

I saw the issue of trust personified in my friends, Tom and Ruth. Tom trusted his ability to provide for his family in a company that appeared to be capable of securing him a stable future. He prepared himself with skills and excelled with a strong work ethic and loyalty to the company. He had done his part, but none of that mattered when they laid him off during an economic downturn. Tom had learned a valuable lesson – only God was completely trustworthy.

Now that Tom is well established and has just a little bit more time on his hands, he stays busy doing things he loves to do, which so often involves helping his fellow believers. One day he is prepping sandwiches for the church's local mission trip. Another day he uses God's resources to buy parts and personally fixes the heating unit in a small country church. I have seen him spend days repairing the steps leading up to the front door of a senior citizen's home, and never even stick around for a thank-you. Doing the right thing for the right reason is enough of a reward for him.

Now Tom's job is managing God's stuff. While others have failed in similar restaurant endeavors, Tom and Ruth have prospered. Yes, hard work has much to do with it, but Tom will be the first to tell you that God is the one who gave him success and God alone gets the glory.

The trust Tom and Ruth put in God allowed them to make a giant leap of faith and has also made them incredibly useful to the advancement of God's kingdom. If you knew them as I do you would see how they fit in the grand scheme of God's plan. The trust they put in God has allowed them to take care of their family and so much more. In a world that is filled with greed there are givers and there are takers. Tom and Ruth are clearly givers who have placed their trust in God.

CHAPTER FIVE

Peace — It's a real thing

You will keep in perfect peace all who trust in you, all whose thoughts are fixed on you!

ISAIAH 26:3

I was a kid in the 60's – a decade of restlessness in America to say the least. Sit-ins and protest marches against discrimination, unemployment, and war. It was a time of rock and roll, hallucinogenic drugs, assassinations, Viet Nam, and the cry of "make love not war." The iconic peace symbol debuted on t-shirts and anti-war posters, and the music of the time shouted "War! What is it good for?" Despite protestors' intentions for peace, the world provided anything but that. Here we are decades later, and the world still hopes for peace, yet when I look around I see so much heaviness, depression, and discontentment pressing down on people, especially those who have filled their lives with stuff.

And that's the problem – people are looking for peace in all the wrong places. Even those who know about Jesus are often tempted to find peace and purpose in temporal things instead of seeking the presence and peace of God. That is why this study began with the foundational truth of God's Divine Ownership and the importance of surrendering your life and all the stuff to Him. As we continue to connect the dots, we will see how affirming God's Divine Ownership gains us access to a deeply trusting spiritual relationship that ultimately brings real peace.

Peace is often associated with joy or moments of temporary happiness, but it is so much more than that. Peace is the calm, the deep-rooted sense of inner serenity when we trust in God's ability, character, and faithfulness. While peace may be impacted by external issues, it is capable of weathering any storm of life because it draws its strength from a divine and supernatural source that enables a believer to be completely at rest in spite of the circumstance. That's how Isaiah could say, *You* {God} *will keep in perfect peace all who trust in you* (Is. 26:3).

I'm sure everyone would agree that there is a shortage of peace in the world today. Global terrorism, school shootings, political unrest, and the list goes on. So, why then at the birth of Jesus, did the angels proclaim peace to the world when they appeared to the shepherds? They filled the night sky saying, *Glory to God in the highest and on earth, peace, good will toward men!* (Luke 2:14, NKJV). Where is that peace and good will?

It's a question that's been asked through the ages. Nineteenth Century poet, Henry Longfellow questioned peace in 1863 amid the Civil War when he wrote, "I heard the Bells on Christmas Day," a poem which referenced the angels' words of peace on earth but goes on to say, "in despair I bowed my head, there is no peace on earth I said; for hate is strong and mocks the song of peace on earth good will to men." Unfortunately, as long as Satan walks the earth, and as long as the hearts of mankind are dark, hate will always be strong, and peace on earth will remain elusive.

In fact, I would say that since Longfellow's sad evaluation, things have continued to go downhill. Based on data from 23 cities homicide numbers are 39 percent higher than they were in 2019. Aggravated assaults and robberies have also increased.[1] Some experts believe the increase is directly related to stress of the COVID pandemic, but personally I think Jeremiah's assessment is more accurate: *The human heart is the most deceitful of all things and desperately wicked. Who really knows how bad it is?* (Jer. 17:9). Because of Satan and darkened human hearts, the paradise that God intended for His creation has become a chaotic jungle.

But God is not a liar, so when His angels announced peace on earth, they had something else in mind. They were announcing a new peace. The peace that comes from reconciliation with God. The peace within that would only be available through that tiny babe in a manger – Emmanuel, God with us. Jesus told his disciples *the peace I give is a gift the world cannot give* (John 14:27). He spoke of an inner peace, the kind that brings complete rest to a weary soul. It is the assurance that the individual has been redeemed and is now at peace with God. It is the comfort of knowing that while things may be unpeaceful in this world, one day all will be well. Apart from salvation through Jesus Christ, this gift of peace is not possible.

PEACE INHIBITORS

The Bible tells stories of people who missed a life of peace because they chose other options over finding peace with their Creator. Belshazzar praised the gods of gold and silver while the handwriting on the wall predicted his demise (Dan. chapter 5). The prodigal son left home with all his riches but ended up in a pig pen far away from peace in his heart (Luke 15:11-32). A rich man had so much that he planned to tear down his barns, build bigger barns, and then eat drink and be merry, but Jesus called him a fool. *You will die this very night.*

Then who will get everything you worked for? Yes, a person is a fool to store up earthly wealth but not have a rich relationship with God (Luke 12:20-21). I think Solomon summed it up nicely by saying, *It is all meaningless – like chasing the wind* (Eccles. 1:14).

There are far too many wind-chasers who choose alternate routes to peace. All these other paths are actually peace inhibitors and as the term implies, a peace inhibitor is anything that prevents an individual from experiencing the gift of peace that Jesus spoke of, and when peace is absent from a person's life, pressure starts to build. Then like a tea kettle blowing off steam, everyday worry and stress will finally explode. We each handle that stress in different ways, so the list of "escape valves" is very personal. The release might be internal and may not be seen by others in the short term, but unresolved stress will always eventually produce explosive results that cannot be hidden. Few things in life cause more stress than financial pressures, but what so many don't realize is that trusting their possessions more than trusting God is just another peace inhibitor. You will never find true peace in your money or other material possessions. Following is a list of some other common things that deter us from the pathway of peace.

WORRY, ANXIETY, AND DEPRESSION

> *Always be full of joy in the Lord. I say it again – rejoice! Don't worry about anything; instead, pray about everything. Tell God what you need and thank him for all he has done.*
>
> PHILIPPIANS 4:4,6

I have always believed that the spiritual battle is fought in the mind. It is there that the deceiver places doubt, shame, anxious worry, and depression, which then leads to behaviors (such as isolation, phobias, or even suicide) based on our thought processes. He has been quite successful in derailing peace in the lives of many. In fact, it is estimated that nearly 264 million people around the globe suffer from depression, and just in the United States, the cost of this disorder is over 210 billion dollars per year! That cost is factored not only from drug treatment, but in hospitalization and missed wages.[2] Depression recently made the list as one of the top five largest contributors of the Global Burden of Disease.[3]

Prescribed medication is a necessary and likely solution, but too often the drugs merely mask the real, deeper issues. Those deeper issues may be anything from DNA to environmental factors requiring intense therapy to reprogram the brain. But it is important to consider the root cause of a troubled soul from a spiritual perspective; otherwise the danger is that only the symptoms are being dealt with by taking prescription drugs. This is not a blanket condemnation of the helpful benefits prescribed by ethical qualified medical and counseling professionals. In fact, there are many within the medical community who include God in the cure and are able to bring real help to hurting people. Medication is often necessary, but I urge you to combine it with *meditation* or focused thinking on God's Word. "No other habit can do more to transform your life...than daily reflection of scripture...you will be amazed at the benefits He has promised to those who take the time to reflect on His Word."[4]

Chinese Christian leader and author Watchman Nee, observed that "An unpeaceful mind cannot operate normally."[5] When one chooses to worry over trusting God, dysfunction follows. Nee proposed that followers of Jesus deliver all anxious thoughts to God as soon as they rise each morning. In 1952, shortly after the Communist takeover of China, Nee was arrested and imprisoned for sharing the Gospel, but his focus was always on the Savior. His faith in God never wavered, and he died completely in God's peace.

Anxiety, depression, and other forms of internal restlessness, clouds the mind and distracts an individual from the true solution, which is to focus on the things of God, and follow Paul's advice: *Dear brothers and sisters, one final thing. Fix your thoughts on what is true, and honorable, and right, and pure, and lovely, and admirable. Think about things that are excellent and worthy of praise. Keep putting into practice all you learned and received from me—everything you heard from me and saw me doing. Then the God of peace will be with you* (Phil. 4:8-9).

EMPTY PHILOSOPHY AND PSEUDO INTELLECTUALISM

And the peace of God, which surpasses all understanding, will guard your hearts and minds through Christ Jesus.

PHILIPPIANS 4:7

One of the surest ways to trouble the soul and destroy inner peace these days is to turn on the television. In this time of political and cultural tension, it's sometimes hard to know which voice to listen to. Paul warned the Colossians not to let anyone capture them with *empty philosophies and high-sounding nonsense that come from human thinking and from the spiritual powers of this world, rather than from Christ* (Col. 2:8). The Bible also says, *Oh, the joys of those who do not follow the advice of the wicked, or stand around with sinners, or join in with mockers* (Psa. 1:1). The only way to defend your mind from today's vain philosophy is to "deny the lie," and recognize it as an attack on your mind, the doorway to your heart - "the strategic place where you determine which seeds are sown and which seeds are discarded."[6] It is vital to guard your heart

128

against worldly lies by fighting to capture every thought that enters your mind and make it submit to God's authority (2 Cor. 10:5). Then you will have a peace beyond human understanding.

Another scam the modern world propagates is found in the lies and claims of academics who believe their knowledge and understanding is better than God's. Without historical or scientific fact, their new understandings are intellectually and socially manufactured responses to God's standards of holiness and personal purity. Paul said in Romans 1:21-22 that *they knew God, but they wouldn't worship him as God or even give him thanks. And they began to think of foolish ideas of what God was like. As a result, their minds became dark and confused. Claiming to be wise, they instead became utter fools.*

Some sincere followers of Christ find it difficult to resist the pseudo intellectual claims of those who have rejected God's laws. Indeed, it can be easy to acquiesce to the dogmatic claims of a professor or a political leader who demands that we accept a new moral code that they claim is based on an intellectually sound social science. Close examination reveals that these radical, manufactured ideas are diametrically opposed to God's loving principles. Therefore, *God abandoned them to do whatever shameful things their hearts desired. As a result, they did vile and degrading things with each other's bodies.*

They traded the truth about God for a lie (Rom. 1:24-25). Because God's standards have been put in place for our own good, it is always wiser to choose the peace of God over the newest views on morality. That's what Paul was talking about in Philippians 4:7. Finding our complete satisfaction in Jesus Christ, brings a peace beyond understanding, and protects our minds from believing the lies of the world.

CONFLICT

Do all that you can to live in peace with everyone.

ROMANS 12:18

Conflict is a definite peace inhibitor. Not to mention that it can cause harmful physical effects such as sleep deprivation, digestive disorders, and even heart disease. In Romans 12:18 Paul encourages us to do our part to get along with other people. That especially applies to our relationship with brothers and sisters in Christ. Pertaining to unity in the body of Christ, we are told to *let the peace of God rule in your hearts* (Col. 3:15). Paul understood that *biting and devouring* could destroy one another (Gal. 5:15), causing great injury to the Church. God's peace within us should be an inoculation against conflict, especially with fellow Christians. That reminds me of a little jingle I once heard on this subject:

To live above with those that we love, that will be glory. But living here below with those that we know, well, that's a different story. (Unknown)

Because Jesus loved us, we are called to love one another, and in doing so, we show the world that we are His followers (John 13:34).

Our actions and attitudes toward others are direct indicators of our Christian status. Scripture tells us not to repay evil with evil or to retaliate with insults even when others insult us. *Instead, pay them back with a blessing. That is what God has called you to do, and he will grant you his blessing. For the Scriptures say, "If you want to enjoy life and see many happy days, keep your tongue from speaking evil and your lips from telling lies. Turn away from evil and do good. Search for peace, and work to maintain it* (1 Pet. 3:9-11).

Search for peace. That's what Jesus meant when he said *blessed are the peacemakers* (Matt. 5:9). He wasn't implying peacemakers are passive people who simply ignore or run away from conflict; but that a peacemaker finds a solution to end the conflict, because conflict destroys peace.

Jesus also said, *If someone slaps you on the right cheek, offer the other cheek also* (Matt. 5:39). What Jesus has asked us to do in turning the other cheek is counterintuitive to everything we know, but the pathway to peace goes much further than just turning your cheek. Jesus asked us to love, bless, and pray for those who mistreat us (Luke 6:27-28). This is what Jesus did for us. Even though He was God, He humbled Himself and bore the pain and shame of the cross. And now we are instructed to have the same humble attitude that Jesus had (Phil. 2:5-8). Clearly, this is not possible when we are at war with others.

INGRATITUDE

One final peace inhibitor is ingratitude. The inability to recognize the blessings you have will trouble your soul and leave you wanting more. But as I've already said, the world's stuff just can't fill the empty spot because it is "a God-shaped hole"[7] and only He can fill it.

Over decades of pastoral counseling, I have found that people who live thankful lives are the most at peace. It's not that their lives are absent of difficulties or trials, but that they have learned to be thankful for what they have and joyfully express gratitude no matter how humble their circumstances. They embraced Paul's advice to Timothy *Afterall we brought nothing with us when we came into the world, and we can't take anything with us when we leave it. So, if we have enough food and clothing, let us be content. But people who long to be rich fall into temptation and are trapped by many foolish and harmful desires that plunge them into ruin and destruction* (1 Tim. 6:7-

9). Paul was right, you can't take it with you. "Ask any coroner. Ask any embalmer. No one takes anything with them. When one of the wealthiest men in history, John D, Rockefeller, died, his accountant was asked, "how much did he leave?" The accountant's reply, "All of it."[8]

Part of the formula for peace and for keeping stuff under control, is to live your life praising God and thanking Him for everything. Whenever greed for more stuff tries to push its way into your life and rob you of peace, thankfulness *in all circumstances* (1 Thess. 5:18) pushes back, and peace prevails. In the cosmic clash between peace and stuff it just makes sense to choose gratitude and find peace every time.

With God's help it is possible to match your wants with your basic needs and live without the press and stress for more and more stuff. Imagine that if the lug nuts holding the wheel on the car are loose, it wouldn't be long before the car starts to wobble. Your life becomes like that car with the loose lug nuts when you lack peace, because your life begins to wobble and eventually the tires fall off. This kind of life is filled with constant turmoil.

The stress and worry that comes from financial realities are common and familiar to everyone who has ever asked the question, "*How much does that cost?*" If you ever hope to bring your worries and even legitimate concerns about finances into check, growing closer to Jesus is the only way for you to grow in your trust of God's goodness. This trust becomes the bedrock foundation of your faith and will always bring peace into your life. This kind of peace is greater than worry, which allows you to conquer your fears. The spiritual growth process that takes place within your heart and mind is not dependent on external circumstances. Fearful and changing conditions in the world around you cannot rob you of the internal peace you have grown through a deep and abiding relationship with Jesus. Since the earliest days of Christianity, people of faith have stood bravely before hungry lions and experienced the presence of Christ in their lives and found Him to be sufficient.

PEACE AND THE PRODIGAL SON

In Luke 15 Jesus told the story of the Prodigal Son. It's the relatable story of a young man who disrespected his father's wishes and demanded that he be given his inheritance so he could leave home and do his own thing. If you are aware of the story, then you know that things did not go well for the ungrateful, rebellious young man. The Bible clearly says *that he wasted all of his money in wild living* (Luke 15:13), never once considering how he might wisely invest his money in something that would last, something that would pay greater dividends. Even something that might be a blessing to others. Instead he selfishly consumed it all on himself.

As the story goes on, a famine swept across the land at the very time that the prodigal's funds ran out, and he found himself in a pig pen. That's *when he finally came to his senses* (verse 17). Abandoned by the friends who were with him when he had money, working a job that he believed to be beneath him, starving, and without hope or peace, his thoughts turned to his father and to all that he had been blessed with. The Prodigal came to the realization that his father loved him. He admitted that he had messed up his life by doing things his own way. To his surprise, when he returned home his father welcomed him back with open arms and threw a banquet to celebrate his return.

The part of the story that people often miss is that the father was never at war with the son. He was waiting to forgive and restore him. Although the Prodigal Son had wasted much of his father's resources, he was thankful to once again be back in his father's house. At last he found peace. The same opportunity is waiting for all who are willing to come home to God. He has blessed us with so much and now it is time to invest those blessings in eternal things and find peace within.

As we close out this chapter on peace, let's go back to Longfellow's Christmas poem claiming that hate was so strong that it mocked the song of peace on earth. We know that much is true, especially against the backdrop of Civil War, the time in which he wrote it. But the poet continued with a hopeful stanza: "Then rang the bells more loud and deep, God is not dead, nor doth he sleep." Yes, no matter what circumstances rage around us, God is wide awake and fully aware of all our challenges, all of our worries and fears; indeed, *the one who watches over you will not slumber* (Psa. 121:3). I pray you will rest peacefully in that wonderful promise. And as you continue reading this book, if you are still struggling with the idea of trusting God with your tithes and offerings, let me just say that you can never outgive the Lord. He is a faithful friend who wants only the best for you. He is good. He is loving. He is kind. He is the *Prince of Peace* (Isa. 9:6).

WHAT DOES PEACE LOOK LIKE?

I mentioned in chapter four how that my wife and I had lots of things in common, but through the years of our marriage we have detected many differences as well. I love football, she never seems to get it; I love mushrooms, but she hates the smell of them, so I rarely get them at home; I love seafood, but again, she hates the smell. She loves to bask in the sun, but when we go to the beach, I'm looking for the biggest palm tree I can find. She loves cats, but I've always been a dog person. The point is we often look at things differently, and sometimes that's a problem that takes some of the peace out of our relationship. But on the other hand, we clearly recognize how God put us together for a purpose, and that is to serve Him in every way that we possibly can.

We make a great team, so when I first felt God leading me to pastor a small church in Northeast Ohio, she was immediately on board. We prayed together about the opportunity and in the summer of 1978 we moved there with our two-year-old daughter, Melinda. Part of our meager salary included living in the church parsonage, located next door to the church. It was a 160-year-old house that had once served as a carriage stop between Canton and Akron. It was complete with four bedrooms, a dining room, a fireplace, and a cellar that might very well have been haunted. These were all things we had never experienced before in our lives and though the house was much in need of repairs, we thought we'd died and gone to heaven. And not having to pay rent was a great blessing, especially when you consider the actual size of that weekly paycheck.

For a while Kathy served as my personal assistant, but when daughter number two came along, I needed to hire someone else for the position. Because I couldn't ask someone to work for free like my wife did, it meant paying another salary, and this little country church just didn't have the funds.

So, once again, we prayed for direction, and soon felt peace about God's leadership in the matter. God led us to give 100 percent of our salary back to the church that week in hopes that it might help make possible the chance to hire an assistant. It was an act of faith. We had so little, and we were about to have another mouth to feed, but still we felt good about the decision. And I have to tell you, God showed up in a big way. The offering that Sunday turned out to be exactly 100 times to the penny of the paycheck we had given.

That, my friends, is no coincidence. God supplied enough to pay that salary for the new staff member for the entire year with money left over for other ministry needs. (You have to understand that the salary was, of course, much, much less that one would expect today.)

Through our short time in that little church God continued to supply in mighty ways. Many of our members were farmers and it was not uncommon to open the back door and discover bushels of fresh corn, beans, and tomatoes. One family raised cattle, and I must say that Kathy and I ate more steak in our tenure there than we ever have since. I also remember needing a new belt, but there just wasn't enough money to go out and buy it, so I explained to God that I needed a new belt and left it with Him. A few days later I was visiting my skinny friend Gene who had accidentally bought a belt that was too big for him, so he asked if I'd like to have it. (Let me say once more that he was very skinny.) Turns out, it was the exact size and even the exact belt that I had previously seen at JCPenney.

Kathy and I believe beyond a shadow of doubt that because we have a Good Shepherd, we have all that we need. He leads us beside peaceful streams, He renews our strength, and guides us along the right paths (Psa. 23). We would be fools not to trust Him.

And because we have honored God from our humble beginnings, He has in return honored us and provided for us beyond what we ever thought possible. He has filled our hearts with a peace that passes all understanding, all we can say is, *Now all glory to God, who is able, through his mighty power at work within us, to accomplish infinitely more than we might ask or think* (Eph. 3:20).

CHAPTER SIX

Usefulness — It's for everyone

*The more you grow like this, the more productive and useful
you will be in your knowledge of our Lord Jesus Christ.*

2 PETER 1:8

Now might be a good time to review this spiritual pathway
we've been traveling. Beginning with the truth that God owns
everything, we've learned that embracing Divine Ownership
comes when we totally surrender our hearts and everything we
possess to Him. From there we experience precious privileges
or blessings that lead us to trust God which then brings inner
peace and contentment into our lives. That spiritually healthy
place of peace opens up the idea of usefulness, which is the
way we *apply* or *use* the resources of God that we steward. Up
to this point we have talked a lot about giving in a financial
sense, but usefulness to God goes far beyond that. We are also

called to be useful or productive with our abilities and talents to expand God's Kingdom here on earth.

The Bible tells us that there is a place of service for everyone in the body of Christ: *All of you together are Christ's body, and each of you is a part of it* (1 Cor. 12:27), but not everyone understands their purpose to be useful. Some people hold back because they feel inadequate, or because selfishly they really don't want to get involved, preferring to come to church unnoticed and slip out the same way. Others have good intentions and seriously want to help but they are still like little children who keep getting the toys out of the toybox but never put the things they played with away. They haven't grown spiritually to understand their part in the body. That is why Paul said, *When I was a child, I spoke and thought and reasoned as a child. But when I grew up, I put away childish things* (1 Cor. 13:11). Scripture makes it clear that a lack of spiritual growth hinders the ability to reach your full usefulness potential.

I gained great insights into the idea of usefulness after reading *The Pioneers*, written by one of my favorite authors David McCullough. As he so often does, McCullough quotes directly from the private journals and public accounts of the historical personalities. By using their own words, he makes each person come alive and it's almost as if you can hear them speaking. *The Pioneers* focused on the first American settlers of the Northwest Territory, which included what would become the states of Ohio, Indiana, Illinois, Michigan, Wisconsin, and the northeastern part of Minnesota. Common to that time in American history there was a specific word used to describe the people who made the most significant contributions toward the welfare of their communities. They were referred to as "useful."

They had come to the new territory prepared to build it by the sweat of their brow. Whether skilled tradesmen, teachers, housewives, or ministers, no one had come along just for the ride. No one had the luxury of idleness, and of necessity, everyone had to pull their weight daily and prove their worth. This standard of community responsibility was part of the moral fabric of a fledgling nation. It was a work ethic that required them to do whatever needed to be done.

Even the children had specific chores because usefulness was taught to them from an early age. Catherine, one of ten children of the pioneering Barker family, recalled that she was raised "to be useful."[1] She also enjoyed quoting her mother's motto:

> *Count the day lost*
> *at which the setting sun*
> *Sees at its close*

no worthy action done.[2]

Playing a part and being useful was a high value of these individuals who sacrificed so much to lay the foundation for this experiment in democracy known as America.

Shortly before the pioneers started crossing the Ohio River, the founding fathers in New England were unselfishly pledging "their lives, their fortunes, and their sacred honors"[3] to carve out a new nation. These professional, wealthy leaders used their education and abilities for the good of others and not just for themselves. One particular example of this is Benjamin Franklin who even chose not to patent many of his inventions (such as the Franklin stove and the lightning rod), because he believed that sharing them was a responsibility he owed to his fellow man. In a 1750 letter to his mother, he wrote that he "would rather have it said that he lived usefully than that he died rich."[4]

Many years later, in his 1961 inaugural address, President John F. Kennedy would challenge Americans to "ask not what your country can do for you – ask what you can do for your country."[5] His words inspired the nation to give themselves to community service and be helpful in meeting the needs of their neighbors. Kennedy's words echo the instructions from Philippians 2:4, *Don't look out only for your own interests but take an interest in others as well.* That kind of unselfishness is not a new thought, and when we unselfishly think beyond ourselves, we have become useful in growing God's spiritual kingdom.

We each have the capacity of being useful and vital to others in the expansion of the Gospel. It is not a concept reserved for the rich and famous, the PhD's, or those who hold political office, but people from every walk of life can and should contribute to their families, churches, and communities. You might say, "But I don't have any skills or special abilities, so what good can I do?" The little boy who shared his lunch comes to mind. With his simple kindness he impacted the lives of thousands that day, and we don't even know his name.

Scripture is full of stories just like that little boy's. Unknown people, perhaps even overlooked, but the value of serving others is evidenced in their actions, even when they themselves were minor players. Their stories didn't make them famous, but you can be sure that God was taking note and because of His view of usefulness, their accomplishments will be rewarded and remembered. I'd like to share a few of their stories with you.

SEVEN BIBLE HEROES YOU'VE NEVER HEARD OF

JEHOSHEBA – 2 KINGS 11:1-3; 2 CHRON. 22:10-11

Athaliah, the daughter of Ahab and wicked Jezebel, was attempting to wipe out all the heirs of King David and end his royal lineage. But Satan's attempt to destroy God's promise of a Savior through David's line was defeated when Jehosheba hid Joash safely in the Temple for six years, until he could be declared the rightful king. The reign of Joash brought revival that turned the nation back to God. Although you may have never heard of Jehosheba before, her actions were useful in fulfilling the prophecy of Jesus our Messiah.

JETHRO – EXODUS 18:13-27

Jethro's story shows us that you don't have to be out front leading to be useful. He was the father-in-law of Moses, the well-known first leader of the nation of Israel. As God pressed upon Moses his calling to lead the Israelites out of slavery, he was overwhelmed with the prospect of such an undertaking. Jethro wisely counseled Moses to delegate the responsibilities of leadership in an organized manner and spread out the weight of the burden. His strategy not only allowed Moses to be the leader God intended him to be, but Jethro's strategies to delegate and break down the monumental task of leadership is still used by businesses and governments today. Jethro remained in the background, but his usefulness made it possible for the leader to complete his calling.

AN UNNAMED SLAVE GIRL – 2 KINGS 5:1-19

This nameless young woman is proof that you need not possess a position or standing to become useful to God. When her master Naaman, a famous and highly decorated Syrian soldier fell ill to the dreadful disease of leprosy, she pleaded with him to go to God's prophet Elisha for healing. He followed her advice and was not only healed but declared his faith and trust in God. This young girl, stolen from her family and living a lowly life of slavery, could have seen Naaman's illness as an opportunity for him to die, but she chose instead to demonstrate love and compassion and as a result, was mightily used by God. His love compels us to show compassion even when others have not shown compassion to us.

SHAMGAR – JUDGES 3:31; AND 5:6

Very little is written about Shamgar in the Bible except that he was a judge in Israel and that during his time, it was perilous to leave the village or even travel on main roads for fear of attack by the ruthless Philistine invaders. Shamgar was a farmer and there is no record that he was ever a mighty military man, but he stepped forward by faith and struck down 600 Philistines with an ox goad, a stick used to prod oxen as they pulled a plow. In the hands of a person of faith that tool was all that was needed to become useful in bringing peace to an entire nation. Shamgar is an example of how the actions of one person can be useful to so many people. As long as you don't mind who gets the credit or whether your name will be remembered, then like Shamgar, you are more than ready to be useful and do miraculous things for God.

ACHSAH – JOSHUA 15:13-19; JUDGES 1:11-15

Caleb, one of the most well-known personalities of the Promised Land story, had a daughter named Achsah, whose name means "courage." Upon evaluation of the land inheritance she and her husband Othniel received, Achsah realized that there was an absence of fresh water, which would make it impossible for her family to live. Though totally living in a patriarchal society, Achsah was unafraid to ask her father for another gift; and because of her bold intercession for those she loved, insured that they would have life-giving water for years to come. From Achsah's example, we see that usefulness is not short sighted, but uses God's courage and wisdom to make good decisions for the future.

EBED-MELECH – JEREMIAH 38:1-13; AND 39:15-18

The name Jeremiah stands out as a bold and courageous prophet who was willing to tell kings and rulers what they did not want to hear. His unpopular message of judgement for those who had rejected God's laws resulted in a contrived plot to have him silenced. Jeremiah was imprisoned in a mud-filled cistern and faced the real possibility of starvation. An Ethiopian man named Ebed-Melech heard that Jeremiah was in the cistern and risked his life to go behind the backs of some powerful government officials to bring his concerns for Jeremiah to King Zedekiah. The king was moved by the case Ebed-Melech made for Jeremiah and allowed him to free God's prophet. Taking into account injuries Jeremiah had sustained during his arrest and imprisonment, he took thoughtful steps to bring comfort to Jeremiah when he removed him from his bondage. He remains today as one of the least known heroes of the faith, but his bravery was useful to an entire nation and made it possible for the well-known prophet to continue his God-given calling. Ebed-Melech's usefulness is impossible to measure.

JOANNA – LUKE 8:1-3; 23:55-56; AND 24:1-12

When Jesus was arrested prior to His staged fake trial and crucifixion, almost everyone who followed Him ran away out of fear for their own lives. But Joanna, the wife of King Herod's business manager, is one of those who faithfully remained for the duration of Jesus's pain and suffering while others abandoned Him. She had often been part of the group that followed Jesus from town to town, and after His death, she was one of the first women to see the empty tomb. Her usefulness in taking the news of Jesus's resurrection to the disciples renewed their faith.

The seven names in these examples are obscure, but each of their stories had a positive impact. Their authentic love for God proved them to be useful in accomplishing His plans and helps us see that even a little can be a lot when it's done for the cause of Christ.

EVIDENCE OF A HEART FOR GOD

Imitate God, therefore, in everything you do because you are his dear children. Live a life filled with love, following the example of Christ. He loved us and offered himself as a sacrifice for us, a pleasing aroma to God.

EPHESIANS 5:1-2

The idea of usefulness is a fundamental theme in the sacrificial life and ministry of Jesus. It defined His life on this earth as He lived and died so that others could be redeemed. *The Son of Man came not to be served but to serve others and to give his life as a ransom for many* (Matt. 20:28).

We are to follow Jesus's example and to be a *pleasing aroma to God.* That is why the value of usefulness must not be overlooked. You are never more like Jesus than when you are serving and following His purposes. It has never been easy to live a life of usefulness in a narcissistic world driven by a "me first" philosophy. Overcoming this selfish compulsion to get all you can is the exact opposite of what Jesus asks His followers to do. As I have so often said, spiritually mature people possess the necessary trust in God to live a life of peace. A peaceful surrendered heart for God is fertile soil that grows a useful, generous life, and becomes *a vessel for honor, sanctified and useful for the Master, prepared for every good work* (2 Tim. 2:21 NKJV).

Some believe that all kingdom work is for pastors or those who have a special calling from God. But that is not true. According to scripture, we are all *God's masterpiece. He has created us anew in Christ Jesus, so we can do the good things he planned for us long ago* (Eph. 2:10).

Paul was God's masterpiece, one of the most devoted and useful followers of Christ in the Bible. But it wasn't always that way. Before his dramatic conversion on the road to Damascus, Paul (previously called Saul) was a well-educated

Pharisee who adhered to the strictest obedience of the Jewish law. By his own words he *was a real Hebrew if there ever was one* (Phil. 3:5). He was zealous in his persecution of the Church, and he obeyed the law without fault. He was very useful in his religious profession, but not in a way that evidenced a heart for God. Not until that bright light changed his life forever (Acts chapter nine), and he realized that all those things that he once considered valuable, were nothing compared to Christ. The apostle then had a new life with new goals. Truly useful goals.

As Paul matured in his faith, he became a major player in God's purposes and was used by God to write half of the New Testament, including this passage from I Corinthians 12:4-7: *There are different kinds of spiritual gifts, but the same Spirit is the source of them all. There are different kinds of service, but we serve the same Lord. God works in different ways, but it is the same God who does the work in all of us. A spiritual gift is given to each of us so we can help each other.*

Did you catch that? *A spiritual gift is given to each of us.* There are no exceptions. Each one of us has been given a gift, a special ability to fulfill our role for God's eternal purposes. *If your gift is serving others, serve them well. If you are a teacher, teach well. If your gift is to encourage others, be encouraging. If it is giving, give generously. If God has given you leadership ability, take the responsibility seriously. And if you have a gift for showing kindness to others, do it gladly* (Rom. 12:7-8).

Without regard for their own welfare, countless people of faith have *gladly* given themselves to sacrificial service. They have surrendered their lives to Jesus and affirmed God's Divine Ownership of their time, talents, and treasures. They understand what it means to be stewards of God's possessions and to have a useful part in ministering to others. This total surrender of all that a person is or possesses is what makes us useful to God's purposes. Why then, when the world's greatest need is for more people to be useful, are there so many among us who have no evidence of usefulness or manifestations of a heart for God?

In very telling ways it seems that many who claim to be followers of Jesus behave more like consumers than useful volunteers. People willing to be useful are rapidly becoming a minority of the Church's population. Somewhere along the way it seems the focus has shifted from selfless behaviors to a mindset that asks, "what can the church do for me?" The world's downward slide to self-indulgence has trickled into many church communities and some people approach the church like passengers on a cruise ship where the hired staff of the ship are there to satisfy their every whim and desire. In some church bodies the takers are outnumbering the givers, leaving the church leadership exhausted and discouraged. Hardly the example of Jesus.

UNLOCKING THE DOOR TO USEFULNESS

And I know that nothing good lives in me, that is, in my sinful nature. I want to do what is right, but I can't. I want to do what is good, but I don't. I don't want to do what is wrong, but I do it anyway.

ROMANS 7:18-19

I've heard it said that one small deed is better than the grandest intention. Can you relate to that? I mean, how many times have you intended to do something, but just never got around to it? What about the times you've been burdened to volunteer for something but failed to follow through? Or when has your heart been moved to give financially to a need you heard of, but something stopped you? The truth is, we don't get any brownie points for just thinking about doing something useful. The ailing widow next door won't enjoy that chicken noodle soup if you don't actually take it to her. The garden won't grow if you fail to plant it. The laundry won't get done if you don't start the washing machine, and the retirement account won't grow if you never invest in it.

Why is that? Why is it that the good things we seriously want to do are the very things that never get done? When your

154

good intentions are derailed from actually happening, you have run into a barrier that stops you from doing what you really felt burdened to do. These barriers take your desires to be useful, productive and turn them into lost opportunities and a whole bunch of regret.

The Parable of the Sower sheds some light on this dilemma. In the story, a farmer planted a field, but some of the seed was eaten by birds; other seed fell on rocky ground; and some seed started to grow, but because the roots were too shallow, the plant wilted in the sun. Jesus used this story to show us that we are so often unfruitful because we are distracted by other things such as *the cares of this world, the deceitfulness of riches, and the desire for other things* (Mark 4:19 NKJV). Though He taught this lesson 2000 years ago, it is still relevant for us today, so it is necessary to find the keys to unlock the doors to usefulness.

1. LOVE GOD

First John 2:15-17 offers us the first key to unlocking usefulness. *Do not love the world or anything in the world. If anyone loves the world, love for the Father is not in them. For everything in the world—the lust of the flesh, the lust of the eyes, and the pride of life—comes not from the Father but from the world. The world and its desires pass away, but whoever does the will of God lives forever* (NIV). As you can tell, this key involves our goals, motivations, and ambitions in life. Take a moment to think about your dreams and passions. Is your love for God greater than your love of the world? Does pursuing things of God have any part in your life or are you pursuing trivial things that will pass away? Remember, God owns everything including the natural gifts and abilities that we were born with, so we need to invest those abilities for kingdom work, be useful, and leave a living legacy for future generations.

2. PUSH AWAY FROM SIN

The second key to becoming useful and productive in the body of Christ is to push away sinful temptations and behaviors. James 1:14-15 says, *those temptations come from our own desires, which entice us and drag us away. These desires give birth to sinful actions.* And sinful actions are definitely not useful. In fact, as in the Parable of the Sower, we are too easily distracted by riches and other things of the world. That's when we end up doing what we didn't want to do. Spiritual seeds can't grow if they are choked and destroyed by sin, rebellion, addictions, and selfish hearts. Perhaps it's time to ask, have I made myself available for God's plans by breaking free from negative sinful behaviors? Have I made myself *useful for the Master, prepared for every good work*? (2 Tim. 2:21).

3. PRIORITIZE

Another key to being useful for Christ is prioritizing our time, talents, and other resources. If we don't plan to put first things first, we won't have time for what is important. Paul taught us to be a living sacrifice (Rom. 12:2), but that will never happen if the things that matter to God never make it on our to-do-list. Are you giving a portion of what God gives you to fund useful ministries? Are you using your spiritual gifts and talents for the benefit of others? Do you manage life wisely, so that you have time to serve when there is a need or a call for volunteers? And perhaps the toughest question of all is "can God trust you?" *And if you are untrustworthy about worldly wealth, who will trust you with the true riches of heaven?* (Luke 16:11).

This kind of spiritual self-awareness is an important step toward becoming a useful servant of our Lord. It is where the privilege of honest self-evaluation comes into play as we strive to keep our priorities in order. It is important to manage our time wisely *because the days are evil,* and to *be not unwise, but understanding what the will of the Lord is* (Eph. 5:16-17

NKJV). We have no promise of tomorrow so the time to be useful in God's plan is now.

4. CONNECT TO A LOCAL CHURCH

The greatest place to apply usefulness is within a local church or body of believers. The Bible instructs us to *not neglect our meeting together as some people do* (Heb. 10:25). If you are not connected to a local church community, you are not fully leveraging your efforts to be useful, because usefulness is amplified when we work together with others in the church body. Your local church is a place where you can grow spiritually, fall deeper in love with God, develop life-long friendships, and partner with others in accomplishing the mission of sharing the Good News. It's a place where God transforms your mind and takes your usefulness to a whole new level. The local church is by far, the most important key for unlocking usefulness. One of the reasons for that is accountability.

Accountability is God's plan to assist us when we feel burdened to make some important changes in our lives, when we need someone to pray with, when we have decisions to make, or even when we're struggling spiritually to stay on the right path. The wicked hearts of humankind prefer darkness but being accountable to someone on a regular basis sheds light on areas of weakness or temptation. Your accountability partner could be a parent, a teacher or pastor, a good friend, or even a spouse. You can also find accountability in a small group where you join with others in Bible discussion and prayer to help you clearly identify your next steps toward growing spiritually and becoming more like Jesus.

The real beauty of connecting to a local church is that flawed and messy people who have been born again, are drawn together to learn about and become reshaped by the only perfect person who has ever lived. That perfect person is, of course, God who came in human form and was known by the name Jesus (John 1:14). His perfection makes possible our transformation from spiritually dead, to spiritually alive. Even though our salvation is immediate when we repent of our sins and call upon the name of the Lord for our salvation, it is only the beginning of our spiritual journey. Our final destination of perfection won't happen until we leave our earthly bodies behind. Growing in Christ is a journey that takes a lifetime and will always be more rewarding and enjoyable in a community of fellow pilgrims.

One of the most powerful benefits of working together with other believers in the local church is the diversity of our gifts and experiences. We need each other to be complete. The abilities and useful resources we have individually, combined with others makes us better together. No one possesses all the abilities or gifts necessary to complete the mission of the Church. We need each other, we need our church, and our church needs us. *We are many parts of one body, and we all belong to each other* (Rom. 12:5).

Paul uses the visual of the human body to help us understand our part in the body of Christ.

Yes, the body has many different parts, not just one part. If the foot says, "I am not a part of the body because I am not a hand," that does not make it any less a part of the body. And if the ear says, "I am not part of the body because I am not an eye," would that make it any less a part of the body? If the whole body were an eye, how would you hear? Or if your whole body were an ear, how would you smell anything? But our bodies have many parts, and God has put each part just where he wants it (I Cor. 12:14-18).

When members of a local church share their gifts with the rest of the body, it is a beautiful thing, resulting in maximized usefulness toward meeting needs and changing lives.

The Apostle Paul understood the benefit of working together. It was his common practice to take his missionary journeys together with other believers who were also surrendered to following the Great Commission. As gifted as Paul was, he clearly saw the value of strategic partnerships. He specifically mentioned a desire to have a young follower of Jesus named Mark join him as he sought to establish new churches in his travels. *Only Luke is with me. Get Mark and bring him with you, for he is useful to me for ministry* (2 Tim. 4:11 NKJV).

The personal enrichment and the relational values of church community are immeasurable but the upside of being a part of a local body to fulfill the mission of the church simply can't be ignored. The work of the Church cannot be accomplished if you try and do it alone, but together with the local body of believers, you have more resources to advance His Kingdom. Your service is more useful because you have the strength of others who will stand with you. Your generosity will have a greater impact because it is combined with others who are surrendered to God's Divine Ownership. In a very tangible way, you become more useful. Please don't forget, your usefulness in fulfilling your part in the Great Commission, gives evidence that you are an authentic follower of Jesus.

THE BIG PICTURE OF CHRISTIANITY'S USEFULNESS

Christ loved the church. He gave up his life for her.
EPHESIANS 5:25

The usefulness of the Church can be measured in the positive impact on people's lives for over 2,000 years. It was always the vehicle by which God planned to spread Christianity throughout the world, beginning in the book of Acts with the call of the first missionary, Paul the Apostle.

The Church has long been the force in changing socially unjust practices, such as the abolition of slavery. William Wilberforce, a member of Parliament as well as a devoted Christian and church leader spent 18 years of his life bringing the teachings of Jesus front and center to outlaw slavery in the British Empire. In 1833, three days after his final bill was introduced to end slavery, he died knowing this evil would no longer be tolerated in Great Britain. The Quakers, and numerous other church groups picked up the spiritually moral responsibility of fighting the violent practice of slavery in America and led in keeping the brutality of enslavement in the public consciousness. Their voice was useful, even essential to the abolitionist cause and was a part of what brought about the needed change.

Then in London in 1844, George Williams founded the YMCA (Young Men's Christian Association) because he feared the effects that poor living and working conditions would have on young men. Seeking to create change, he established Bible study groups that fostered healthy living and provided a safe environment to contrast life in the streets. Organizations such as Alcoholics Anonymous, rooted in faith principles, were also designed to bring about life change. Christian schools have been established, hospitals and orphanages have been brought into existence, all to counteract the hate and destruction brought on by Satan's vicious agenda.

The usefulness of the Church has been instrumental in reforming prisons, creating better working conditions and changes in labor abuses. It has provided medical care in both natural disasters and during the conflict of war. Countless charities have been established. The Red Cross, Salvation Army, Samaritan's Purse, International Fellowship, and countless other non-profit organizations have been staffed and funded by Christians as they follow the example of Jesus and care for the broken people of our world.

In most American communities it would be rare if you could not find at least one hospital that traced their roots back to the Church. Schools and universities, foodbanks, and countless other community services have intricately been intertwined with faith-based Christian communities. The usefulness of the army of church volunteers has provided the labor and the funds that fueled everything from orphanages to rescue missions. It is hard to imagine the vacuum that would exist if the Church had not served as a launching pad for inspiration and useful action.

It is impossible to measure all the benefits that the Church has provided through the centuries. Because the change that takes place in the lives of those transformed by the Gospel happens within the heart, the world outside the Church rarely takes notice. But the truth is, transformed people of God are useful to transform the world. The orphaned child who now has a home certainly has noticed. The spouse whose marriage relationship has been restored because of the transformative power of Jesus has no doubt taken note. The evil that never happened because of the people who were converted and changed by Jesus are rarely talked about but those who served and gave to make these miracles possible have been useful beyond measure.

From its conception until now, the greatest usefulness of the Church has been to share Christ's love with the lost world. If you believe God is real and that your redemption was purchased by the sacrificial death of Jesus, you can be born again. Then you can live your life with the meaningful purpose of making the world a better place. We all have been commissioned to go, we are all called upon to give. That may mean giving your life in full-time service, or simply investing and volunteering in your local church. Affirming Divine

Ownership allows you to trust Him completely. No more worries, no more fear, your life is in His hands. The proof of all this is your usefulness to God's purposes and His plans for the world.

WHAT DOES USEFULNESS LOOK LIKE?

They even did more than we had hoped, for their first action was to give themselves to the Lord and to us, just as God wanted them to do.

2 CORINTHIANS 8:5

So often the idea of stewardship is in the context of giving money, but we need to understand that Divine Ownership is also about giving our time and talents to be useful for God's purposes. Many wonderful people volunteer in their local church on a regular basis, but then there are some who fully embrace the value of *sacrificially* giving themselves to the mission of the Church, and in doing so their service revolutionizes an entire church community. That is exactly what Bob, Howard, Duane, George, Dave, and Rick did when they sacrificed nearly a year of their lives to a project that made a dated and neglected facility useful once again. Their efforts contributed greatly to the rebirth of a local church and the facility they worked on was made ready to facilitate God's kingdom work.

All now retired from various careers, one had been the VP of a successful company, another a maintenance engineer. There was also a former law enforcement officer, an electrician, one with a career in a lumber and home improvement chain, and another worked in manufacturing. All had recently earned the right to slow things down and do some of what they had looked forward to their entire work careers. The bucket list of things to do, however, would have to wait because God burdened each of them to give themselves to the full-time grind of showing up to work every day without pay. Each would use their gifts and individual abilities to launch a church into God's preferred future.

Besides these six, other volunteers came as often as they could to paint, clean-up workspaces, or to provide lunch for all the volunteers. Many men, women, and even children responded to calls of "all hands on deck." Everyone made a difference. Still, the backbone of the effort was the six faithful daily workers who pressed on, contributing unlimited hours of their time all the way to the building dedication. The repurposing of an existing building with a limited budget was a daunting challenge, virtually every inch of the newly purchased property needed attention. New ceilings, new lights, new cabinets, and trim everywhere in the building. A completely new heating and cooling system was necessary, signage, painting, the parking lot and new landscaping – the list goes on and on. Floor coverings were removed and new installed, some walls were moved, others were completely taken out, restrooms were gutted, and new plumbing was installed. New windows and insulation to reduce energy costs would allow future giving to be used entirely for ministry efforts.

The brave decision to undertake the relaunch of the church had received unanimous support from the congregation and everyone was doing their part, but these six guys did something extraordinary. Yes, there was an entire church unified in a miraculous faith effort, but these men allowed God to use them to make possible something that, humanly speaking, could not have happened without their sacrifice. Their volunteer labor freed up hundreds of thousands of dollars to purchase the materials for the project to be completed with excellence. And, just in case you are wondering, no money was borrowed, no debt was taken on by the church, everything would be paid for the day the new gathering place for the church body was dedicated.

The gift of these faithful stewards allowed an entire faith community to get a new start and hit the ground running with vibrant ministries that continue to this day advancing the mission Jesus gave His Church. They never received compensation for their good deeds, their names will never appear in the bold print of a news article, and now years later, their incomparable usefulness of that time is a past memory. They had been useful to God in an extraordinary way, and only He (and their families) really knows the extent of the sacrificial gift they gave. Embracing Divine Ownership, these six men fully believed that their abilities were *from* God and *for* God. They showed us what usefulness looks like when people not only give financially, but also give their lives for something bigger than self. This is a gift God has called each of us to give and those who choose to make this offering will find that the blessings and eternal rewards they receive are far beyond the worth of anything the temporary stuff of this world can give.

CHAPTER SEVEN

Generosity – It's who you are

*But generous people plan to do what is generous, and they
stand firm in their generosity.*

ISAIAH 32:8

Maybe like me, you've met some people with "alligator arms."
That means that their arms are too short to ever reach into
their pockets to help someone in need. They are selfish,
stingy, with hearts of stone that never seem moved with
compassion. The truth is the world could use a few more
unselfish, generous people – people like Francis Chan.

Chan had been on the mission field in Africa and upon
his return to the States felt God leading him to sell their
family's house and move into a smaller house for the purpose
of having more funds available to give away. He told how
others advised him not to do this – that it was a bad financial
plan. Some even questioned his motives, that he was just

trying to make himself look good. But the Chan family followed God's leading, and they have never regretted it. In the context of eternity, Chan asks, "Am I the crazy one for selling my house? Or are you for not giving more, serving more, being with your Creator more?"[1]

Now that is generosity!

In our last chapter we talked about how usefulness is evidence of your growing relationship with God. Your faith is deeper, your trust in God more secure. It should not surprise you then that there are also natural connections between spiritual growth and generosity, which becomes the fuel that drives the engine of more usefulness and keeps God's purposes moving forward.

Looking back to the early days of my Christian faith, I can now clearly see how at the age of 17, a bodacious act of generosity brought about a quantum leap in my faith. I could not explain it at the time, but something had changed. Like any high school senior, I had normal questions about my new found faith, resulting in some struggles mostly influenced by typical desires to have more stuff. Stuff was trying to own me, but my new faith was asking me to make Jesus Lord of my life over the desires for stuff. This storm of inner conflict blew into my life, testing my new life in Jesus.

After crossing the line of faith and asking Jesus to save me, I declared my relationship with Him in public baptism. Less than three weeks later a missionary (whose name I can now not even remember) spoke at the church I attended. The images he showed on the screen, the stories he told, the needs he described moved my soul like nothing had ever moved me before. The Holy Spirit now living in me was speaking to my heart and bringing me face to face with the real meaning of generosity. This missionary asked for financial help to continue taking the Gospel to people who needed what I had just received when I accepted Christ into my life just a few weeks earlier. The internal anguish that ensued from the request of this missionary brought storm waves of financial conflict to me. I did not have any money to give him, I could barely put gas in my car. What would I do with this new awareness of need and the undeniable sense of responsibility and compassion that I was feeling?

I remember praying in a manner that was radically different than any prayer I had ever prayed before. There was an authentic urgency to what I felt, and I could not get it out of my head. But I had no money to give, and no way of getting my hands on any either. It was football season, the one time of the year that I didn't work a job after school hours or weekends. It seemed reasonable to me that I would not be able to give to this missionary's need; but the nagging sense of urgency about it would not go away. The people of the church had been instructed to take the missionary offering material home and pray for a week then return the offering promises to church the following Sunday. So, I took the information home thinking that will be the last of that, and in a way the pressure was off. I was pretty sure there would be nothing I could do.

But then I saw the sign.

A sign that said HELP WANTED could be seen from the window of a greasy spoon restaurant I passed on my way home from church the day the missionary spoke, and it kept popping up in my mind. At first it was easy to dismiss it, football season was in full swing, there was just no way for me to handle a job with the demands of practice and the all-consuming impact that Friday night lights had on my life. But then every time I drove by that crazy sign the voice of that missionary was ringing in my ears. Noticing that haunting sign for the third time, I pulled into the parking lot, turned off my car, and entered a whole new unfamiliar struggle. God was speaking to me, and I wasn't sure I liked it. I wanted the voices of the missionary and the Holy Spirit to go away. I wanted to forget about the images on the screen. I wanted them to disappear, but they would not. Sitting in my 1965

Mustang, I prayed a prayer that would change my life. I promised God I would work if the hours fit into my impossible schedule. I felt a bit of relief because I was certain that when I went in and asked about the hours available that it would not be humanly possible to fit them into my schedule, and I would be off the hook. But I could not have been more wrong.

When I asked the woman on the other side of the counter what the hours were for the job attached to that irksome sign, she said it was Friday and Saturday nights from 10:00 p.m. until 6:00 a.m. We talked for a few moments and then she asked me if I wanted the job. That Friday night after the football game, I quickly cleaned up, got in my car and drove to the greasy spoon restaurant and worked the graveyard shift. When the local bars closed at two a.m., the all-night restaurant came alive. Surrounded by the smell of drunken motorcycle club members and the greasy hamburgers, I began to question my sanity. But in the middle of it, I felt an odd sense of serenity, certain that I was doing what God had pressed upon my heart to do. The searing image of the sign no longer kept me awake and the nagging words of the missionary were replaced with a sense of purpose and peace. After working that second night, I showered away the smell of the greasy burgers and went to church on Sunday morning with the promise card in hand. And there in my own handwriting was a specific number beside a dollar sign.

A few weeks later my church collected the offerings promised for the missionary's project. The 50 dollars that I gave represented every penny I had made leading up to that offering. Working 16 hours each weekend at a wage of 1 dollar an hour took me over a month to earn what I had felt burdened to give. The struggle I went through resulting in my commitment to give generously did became a foundational and a defining moment in my life. From that time forward the process of listening to God and trusting Him to guide all my giving decisions would always be my future practice. I experienced what it was to trust God and I found the deep satisfaction of being generous. He allowed me to be part of something bigger than myself. Although I did not know how to describe it then, I realize now that my faith had been activated. I found out how meaningful it could be to have a part in what God was doing in a country I had never been to and touch the lives of people I did not even know.

I have wondered over the years how different my life would have turned out if I had silenced the press against my heart to help that missionary. It is true for you as well, that leaning *into* those moments when God speaks to your heart, instead of ignoring His voice, will pave the way for future giving. So, for the next few pages we are going to look at the revolutionary concept of generosity that Jesus so often talked about and discover how practicing generosity can change your life and make you a generous person.

WHAT GENEROSITY IS NOT

I tell you the truth," Jesus said, "this poor widow has given more than all the rest of them. For they have given a tiny part of their surplus, but she, poor as she is, has given everything she has.

LUKE 21:3

Jesus had a standard for measuring generosity, and it had nothing to do with the size of a gift, because generosity in God's economy is not measured by how much you give but by how much you have left after you give. In the story of the widow's mite, Jesus teaches us that the small amount called a *mite,* given by the widow was more than anyone else's gift. The Jewish *mite,* also called the Greek *lepta,* was the smallest coin in circulation at the time Jesus was teaching this lesson in the Temple. In those days, the mite represented the smallest possible fraction of a day's wages, about 1/8 of a cent in today's currency.[2]

Are you getting your head and heart around this? Giving in God's economy is valued by the sacrifice which is an indication of the heart condition. This story about the widow is even more humbling when you consider that the religious braggarts there in the Temple were giving much larger amounts, but their gifts were not on the scale of sacrifice as was the widow's. Their giving was to be seen by others. These pompous hypocrites had missed the whole idea of what stewardship is about. They never grasped the fact that all of the stuff really belonged to God and that giving was a heart issue not a currency issue.

To help you see what I mean, let's take a look at a survey of giving by some of the world's richest people. I'm not trying to diminish their charity or render judgement, but merely putting into context how God measures generosity. I'll just give you the numbers and let you draw your own conclusion, using the same standard Jesus used when he said the widow had given more than anyone else.

Of the 400 billionaires on the Forbes list of the world's wealthiest people, 156, gave less than 1 percent of their wealth to charity. On the same list, just 19 gave away more than 10 percent of their wealth. That means that 381 of the world's wealthiest people did not even give a tithe of their wealth to help others.[3] Not only do the wealthiest among us give proportionally less than those who possess significantly less, but they are less happy. A series of studies conducted by Paul

Piff and his colleagues from the University of Berkeley, involved a game of monopoly which revealed that the richer a player grew in the game, "the meaner he/she progressively became," assuming more dominant postures as the game progressed. Piff further claims that one of the reasons that the wealthy are less generous is that wealth has made them more isolated. The study suggests that their wealth contributes greatly to their lack of meaningful relationships and *has a deleterious effect on happiness.*[4]

Remember, according to Jesus, generosity is not defined by how much you give. A person who gives away millions but still has billions left should not be considered a sacrificial person or even a generous person for that matter. This observation is not meant to demean any gift given by any person for any amount. It is only intended to help you understand that you can be generous even though you do not possess significant wealth. The faith required to give as God leads, means fully trusting in God's goodness and believing that giving our gifts is for advancing the Good News of Jesus and everlasting life change.

GENEROSITY IS FAITH IN ACTION

And I am praying that you will put into action the generosity
that comes from your faith as you understand and experience
all the good things we have in Christ.

PHILEMON 1:6

I've always found that listening to stories of generous people builds my faith. Hearing how God provided for them when they made generous sacrifices fires up my own faith and inspires me to greater generosity. They all say the same thing, that their faith and generosity started small, but continued to grow. Each act of faith was a building block or a steppingstone to even greater faith enabling them to be more useful, generous people.

The shepherd boy David is another example of someone who first exercised small faith but later accomplished courageously impossible deeds. Before he ever had the faith and courage to face the giant Goliath, David had first trusted God to help him protect his father's sheep from wild animals. I can almost imagine him kneeling down on the rug made from the hide of the predator he had killed defending his family's livestock to pray before he fought Goliath. And likewise Moses at first stepped out with fear to confront Pharoah, but soon became the leader who confidently raised his staff and parted the waters of the sea.

The greater your faith in God, the greater your ability to be generous, so allowing God to use you first in small ways opens your eyes to the potential of what can be. Paul prayed for others to be more generous because he had experienced the power of generosity himself and passionately wanted others to experience this fulfilling part of being a Christian. He knew that people who put their faith and trust in Jesus, had the potential to also be generous.

Transforming natural impulses from thinking of ourselves first to refocusing attention on the needs of others isn't a change you can just instantly pull off on your own, because of the natural "me first" mentality. But what is natural is not necessarily spiritual, so this transformation is only possible when you have the Spirit of Christ living within. Transformation will happen, but you must first take baby steps before becoming a generous giver. So, there is no need to stress about giving, just keep trusting God and as your faith grows, you will soon be moving mountains (Matt. 17:20).

The Bible tells us that when we come to Christ, we *become a new person. The old life is gone; a new life has begun!* (2 Cor. 5:17). Your new spiritual DNA is programed by God to take your old parts and make them into something beautiful and new. This amazing change that takes place is more remarkable than when the caterpillar morphs into a beautiful butterfly. The same God who transforms the butterfly, wants to transform you into something beautiful. He wants you to become a person of generosity. Like the new butterfly breaking free from the chrysalis, you can also break free from financial bondage and selfishness. You have been charged with setting your thoughts on the eternal rather than on the decaying things of this world. So, your part in this transformation is to open your heart and mind to the promises God has made that with Him *nothing would be impossible* (Matt.17:20).

GENEROSITY THRIVES IN AN UPWARDLY FOCUSED LIFE

Set your mind on things above, not on things on the earth.
COLOSSIANS 3:2 NKJV

I focus on this one thing: Forgetting the past and looking forward to what lies ahead.
PHILIPPIANS 3:13

What you focus on is a choice. Where you allow your mind to dwell is a critically important decision that you make many times every day. A dieter has to stop mentally dwelling on the cookies in the pantry; the man with financial problems must refocus his thoughts or he is prone to stay awake with worry; and the woman suffering from the shame of her past must stop listening to the wrong voice in her head. To a large extent, we become what we allow our minds to think about. And what we think about affects our behavior. So, doesn't it make sense that thinking about others could make us more generous?

Concentrating on the right things requires commitment and discipline because our hearts are so often distracted, scattered. We become "suckers for the latest craze or quick fix. This project, then another. Lives with no strategy, no goals, no defining priorities."[5] Shiny objects (such as our phones) catch our attention and divert our focus to matters that are mundane and meaningless, preventing us from listening to the Spirit within. "Most people go through life thinking God never speaks to them when in fact He's always speaking. But we hear so little of what He says because our consciousness of His voice is obscured by mental static."[6] What you focus on – what voice you listen to – is not a one and done choice, but a decision you have to make many times every day.

Besides being a choice, the ability to focus is an acquired skill. In some ways we all have the attention span of a cat, or a type of spiritual ADD. (Cat lovers, I mean no disrespect.) People's inability to focus continues to worsen in today's modern world. It may be hard to believe but the average human attention span has decreased by nearly 25 percent since the year 2000. The average person now has an attention span of just 8.25 seconds, lagging behind the goldfish which stands at 9 seconds.[7] It's no wonder that we have a hard time locking in on a single thought or subject when the world is coming at us from so many different directions from the moment we wake up until we try to fall asleep at night.

But thinking on the things of God is an important practice when it comes to generosity. Scripture says *do not be conformed to this world but be transformed by the renewing of your mind* (Rom. 12: 2). The potential for a transformed mind is exclusively found in Jesus. When we experience that new birth in Christ, the Holy Spirit indwells us and gives us the power to not only renew our minds but to *stay* focused on spiritual things as well. As our Comforter, He calms our fears and guides our thinking – if we will listen to His voice.

We have a granddaughter who is quite demonstrative and has no problem voicing her opinions. Sometimes that gets her into a pinch with her mom. So, when Mom needs to get *her* opinion across, she gently takes her daughter's chin in her hand and says, "Look at me. I need to see your eyes." Eye contact ensures that she is listening to her mother. It's true for us as well. God needs to see that our minds' eyes are focused on Him. It's how He knows we are listening.

Paul struggled with the way his mind worked because of the sin nature that he still carried around in his body. *I love*

God's law with all my heart. But there is another power within me that is at war with my mind. This power makes me a slave to the sin that is still within me (Rom. 7:22-23). The source of sin's power over us starts in the form of the enemy's deception in the mind. Satan distorts God's truths by adding a little something to it. So, it is no longer God's truth, but a believable deception to anyone who isn't completely focused on God. Paul warned the Colossians, *Don't let anyone capture you with empty philosophies and high-sounding nonsense that come from human thinking and from the spiritual powers of this world, rather than from Christ* (Col. 2:8).

A large host of self-help authors will tell you how important it is to change the way you think but as Paul warned, beware because they all reject the most fundamental truth that only Jesus Christ can transform us and heal our minds. Tony Robbin's *Unlimited Power* suggests that by tapping into the power of our mind, we can be, do, have, achieve, and create anything we want in life.[8] Eckert Tolle's book *The Power of Now* is a guide to spiritual enlightenment (and one of Oprah's favorites).[9] Then there's Gary Zukav who claims that our souls have incarnated so that we might fulfill missions and continue to evolve.[10] That's not what Jeremiah said: *The human heart is the most deceitful of all things, and desperately wicked. Who really knows how bad it is?* (Jer. 17:9).

Yet, these false teachers continually lead others to look within a sin sick soul instead of looking to Jesus, and only Jesus can *restore* the soul (Psa. 23:3 NKJV).

Many other New Age gurus flood talk shows, blogs, or podcasts and ambitiously saturate bookstores with their self-help psychobabble, but they all are making the same mistake. They think finding the answers to life's questions are found by looking within ourselves. They may use spiritual words and occasionally even talk about Jesus, but none of them will tell you that Jesus alone is the answer to a changed heart and soul. They may talk about soulful awakenings, but anyone who rejects Jesus above all, is offering fool's gold which in this case *sounds* good but has no real value. Keep in mind Shakespeare's saying, *all that glitters is not gold*, meaning that what appears valuable on the surface, may in fact, be deception.

An upward focus on Jesus and a deeper knowledge of God's Word will help you discern His truth from a lie. Proverbs 4:23 says to *Guard your heart above all else for it determines the course of your life*. When God's truth is "out of focus" in your life, or if a half-truth trips you up you are vulnerable to moving your mind to deceptive humanistic thinking. Paul reminded the Colossians that Christ must have preeminence in a Christian's affections and worship. He said to *Set your mind on things above, not on things on the earth* (Col.

3:2 NKJV). It is our upward focus on *things above* that creates within us a desire for others over the desire for self. It is the spiritual fruit of our walk with Christ that can make us a radically generous person.

Those consumed by a desire for more, never fully see the needs of others through the fog of their own greed. Their love for worldly things has blinded them. The remedy for a self-focused view of life is looking to Jesus. The closer we get to Him, the more clearly, we see Him, the more we will desire to be generous. Our focus will shift from stuff to people, and we will see the value of generosity and those things that are closest to the heart of God. If you want to know where your heart really is, refocus your attention, follow the money, because where *your treasure is, there the desires of your heart will also be* (Matt. 6:21).

GENEROSITY REQUIRES A PURE MOTIVE

When you give to someone in need, don't do as the hypocrites do—blowing trumpets in the synagogues and streets to call attention to their acts of charity! I tell you the truth, they have received all the reward they will ever get.

MATTHEW 6:2

One final cautionary thought about generosity is the danger of wrong motives. God looks at the heart, not the outward appearance, so giving from a generous heart is the goal, not giving because we feel coerced or because we want to signal our virtue. Jesus spoke harshly to the Pharisees because He knew their hearts were dark. They were leaders of the Jewish law, but though God in the flesh stood before them, they were too blind to see Him. He knew that their public giving was nothing more than an act, and not a heartfelt desire to please God. Giving for attention that inflates one's ego or status will not result in God's favor or any eternal rewards.

In the first days of the Church, a number of members stepped forward and sold everything they had and gave all the money to meet the needs of the struggling new church. The care of the widows who had been receiving support from their previous connection to Judaism, was of special concern to the new church because these elderly women who had followed Jesus were now unable to take care of themselves. There was a need, and the early Christians *were one in heart and mind. No one claimed that any of their possessions was their own, but they shared everything they had* (Acts 4:32). No one had been commanded to sell everything they possessed, but people were doing this because of extraordinary generosity. Remember, Ananias and Sapphira, enamored by the acclaim others had received for being generous, wanted the attention and credit for making a similar sacrifice, so they lied and said the money they were giving was everything they had received from the sale of their property. This lie led to their demise and is an important lesson about the evil of giving with false motives. It is a somber warning about taking credit for something you did not do, and the principle remains today that generosity must be pure to be honored by the One who gave His all for us.

I have found that generous people are spiritually sensitive, not stingy or selfish. When someone's heart is tuned-in to Jesus, they can sense when there are needs and are open to His leading. They have discovered that everything in this world is not about them or for them. They have found that a giver's joy lasts longer than the goosebumps they get from buying more stuff. They understand that giving, not getting, is the way.

Luke 15 tells the stories of three things that were lost: a sheep, a coin, and a son. In each story, there was great rejoicing when the items were finally found, but Luke tells us that heaven also rejoices when a lost sinner comes to God. Whether we personally go out and seek the lost or generously fund the efforts to reach them, we are all part of that celebration.

Well done, good and faithful servant (Matt. 25:21) are the words we all want to hear from God someday, so to keep our motives on track, here are just a few scriptural references to show us what generosity looks like when we give with a pure heart motive.

- Pure hearted generosity sees the material needs of people and freely gives. *They share freely and give generously to those in need. Their good deeds will be remembered forever. They will have influence and honor* (Psa. 112:9).

- Pure hearted generosity comes from a faith that knows Christ. *And I am praying that you will put into action the generosity that comes from your faith as you understand and experience all the good things we have in Christ* (Philem.1:6).

- Pure hearted generosity would rather give than get more stuff. *Some people are always greedy for more, but the godly love to give!* (Prov. 21:26).

- Pure hearted generosity never gives grudgingly but with a joyful heart. *Give generously to the poor, not grudgingly, for the Lord your God will bless you in everything you do.* (Deut. 15:10).

- Pure hearted generosity knows it is far greater to give than receive. *You should remember the words of the Lord Jesus: 'It is more blessed to give than to receive* (Acts 20:35).

- Pure hearted generosity comes from a heart that is clean. *Then the Lord said to him, "You Pharisees are so careful to clean the outside of the cup and the dish, but inside you are filthy—full of greed and wickedness! Fools! Didn't God make the inside as well as the outside? So, clean the inside by giving gifts to the poor, and you will be clean all over* (Luke 11:39-41).

THE BLESSINGS OF BECOMING A GENEROUS PERSON

Jesus taught that the pure in heart would see God (Matt. 5:8). When our sins have been washed away, when all the stuff of this world is no longer our ambition, when our motives have been purified we truly "see God." We clearly see His heart and the need for the lost world to see Him also. Living is no longer about accumulating more stuff, but about reaching others, so when we give with a pure heart blessings follow such as those listed below.

- The generous will be blessed by God because they cared for those in poverty. *Blessed are those who are generous because they feed the poor* (Prov. 22:9).
- The generous will be refreshed by God. *The generous will prosper; those who refresh others will themselves be refreshed* (Prov. 11:25).

- The generous will have God's light for the darkness of this world. *Light shines in the darkness for the godly. They are generous, compassionate, and righteous* (Psa. 112:4).

- Generous people cause others to glorify God. *As a result of your ministry, they* {others} *will give glory to God. For your generosity to them and to all believers will prove that you are obedient to the Good News of Christ* (2 Cor. 9:13).

- The generous invest wisely and have stored up treasures in heaven. Jesus said, "*Don't store up treasure here on earth where moths eat them and rust destroys them, and where thieves break in and steal. Store your treasures in heaven, where moths and rust cannot destroy, and thieves do not break in and steal. Wherever your treasure is, there the desires of your heart will also be*" (Matt. 6:19-21).

There are many immediate blessings for those who live generous lives, but nowhere in the above passages are you promised the blessing of a bigger house or more money in your bank account, because those are not the things that matter. Sadly, many are still too consumed with the pursuit of stuff to understand this and will one day be filled with sorrow and regret that they did not do more to ease the suffering of others. It is a humbling thought. This deeply troubling concept is described in the book *Schindler's List*, which became an award winning movie.

Set in World War II, in Nazi occupied Poland, there is a scene early in the movie where Nazi party member, Oskar Schindler, is celebrating his birthday with a group of other Nazis in a nightclub. The excessive waste of money spent for the celebration stood in dramatic contrast to the evils of the Holocaust just outside the party. Schindler was part of that cruelty and barbarism because he profited from the free, harsh labor of the Jews. It would not be until he personally witnessed the horrific brutality of the Nazi regime that he experienced a kind of awakening. Not only was he then aware of the truth of what was going on, but he instantly came to the realization that he was a part of the evil. By looking the other way and doing nothing, he had been an active participant in the savagery.

From that awakening moment, Schindler was driven to spend his significant wealth to purchase the lives and freedom of those from whom he had previously profited. The workers in his factory were no longer cogs on a machine that manufactured his profits, they had become people who mattered. In the days that followed, Schindler used his pull within the Nazi party and his own resources to save the lives of more than 1000 Jewish individuals who worked in his Polish factory. From there he would purchase the documents necessary to facilitate their escape. At the end of the movie, Schindler, even though he is financially ruined and a war criminal running from the Allies, has an emotional breakdown. He looks around at all the people he rescued, but says, "I could have done more…I could have saved more but I didn't."[11]

Schindler's haunting words make us wonder what we are doing as stewards of God's resources and ask ourselves whether we should be doing more. God may never ask us to physically rescue innocents from hateful regimes, but we have been commanded to rescue souls from spiritual darkness. Are we really trying to do that in a generous way? The Church has survived and thrived for 2,000 years because generous people who lived before us gave their lives and resources so the truth about Jesus could be heard in our generation. Now, it is time for us to carry the love of Jesus through ministries of care and compassion. It is up to us to make sure everyone knows that because Jesus conquered death, they can have eternal life and we can take our place as beacons of generosity.

RADICAL GENEROSITY

And all the believers met together in one place and shared
everything they had. They sold their property and possessions
and shared the money with those in need. They worshiped
together at the Temple each day, met in homes for the Lord's
Supper, and shared their meals with great joy and generosity
all the while praising God and enjoying the goodwill of all the
people. And each day the Lord added to their fellowship those
who were being saved.

ACTS 2:44-47

I can't imagine any greater demonstration of generosity than
the selfless act of selling all your stuff and giving the money
away to those in need within your community of faith. To me
it seems like the faith equivalent of jumping off a cliff without
a parachute. They generously gave away their certainty of a
next meal and chose to trust God for their own daily bread so
that others could be fed.

I know this sounds incredibly radical to us today, but
before you close this book and say, the author has gone a
bridge too far by even referencing the extreme generosity of
the first church in Jerusalem, let me put it into context. Jesus
had just conquered death by rising from the dead, and the
participants in this radical generosity were eyewitnesses to His
crucifixion and resurrection. Present at this church gathering
were people who had walked and talked with Jesus during the

three-and-a-half years of His earthly ministry. These people who gave away everything trusted Jesus because they had been touched by Him and had witnessed His miracles.

Have we not also been touched by the Savior?

Just to be perfectly clear as we discuss the sacrifices of these early Christians, no place in scripture are we asked to sell everything and give it to our local churches. But the story does provoke a deeper look within our own hearts and cause us to question why we might have difficulty surrendering even ten percent back to God. Afterall, the stuff we have all belongs to Him to begin with, and the same faith of the early followers of Jesus is the same faith we have available to us.

When you truly become a generous person focused on what matters to God, you see that the most important things in life don't have a price tag. Deeper relationships, less anxiety over what you don't have, and a new appreciation for what you do have are possible as you experience the blessings of a generous heart. A life of generosity is proof that you have an authentic relationship with Jesus and that you truly believe in God's Divine Ownership. As a steward of God's possessions, you serve as His hands in bringing love and peace to the hopeless. I can't imagine that anyone will ever stand before God one day and look back with regret because they lived a life of generosity.

Does God still love you if you are not a giver? Yes, He does, but there is so much more in store for you if you are willing to follow His giving principles. Once again, it must be stressed that knowing the heart of God through a deep and abiding relationship with Him is the foundation of your ability to trust Him. Knowing Him allows you to see that He would never ask you to do anything that will harm you. Your privileged relationship with God opens your eyes to the value of surrendering to His Divine Ownership, the premise upon which all scriptural giving principles are built.

WHAT DOES GENEROSITY LOOK LIKE?

I remember so clearly the first time I met Rick Schuessler. He and I were both freshman students in college and one day as we passed each other walking to class, I saw Rick smile. It was a smile I have seen a thousand times since, but I'll never forgot the first time I saw it. You see, only two years earlier, over 35 percent of Rick's body had been burned in a tragic fire including the entirety of his face. I later learned that he had personally escaped unscathed from the fire, and that most of his injuries occurred when he repeatedly went back inside a burning cabin to rescue others.

Months and years of the painful recovery included multiple surgeries, skin grafts, and various therapies. But Rick was determined to show everyone that "there is someone inside this scarred, mutilated body that is far different than the one they see."[12]

Courage, bravery, hero, are all words that come to mind when I think of Rick. Beneath all the burnt scar tissue there is a person who is loving and caring, a man who is a giver, a person of generosity. Running into a burning building and giving so much of his life for others was not just what he did, it's who Rick is. On that day we first passed each other on the sidewalk, I had no idea that he would not only become a dear friend, but he would come to personify what sacrificial love and generosity are all about.

As young men in our 20's, Rick and I pastored churches in Toledo, Ohio. The city was often called "holy Toledo" because there were so many churches there, and our churches were a mere 1.9 miles apart. Being so close together we were able to grow our friendship. Looking back, I think for me, the greatest blessing was to witness Rick's generosity and selfless service in everything he did. It was a humbling thing and inspired me to be more like Jesus.

Rick's selflessness was also apparent through all the legal proceedings related to the fire. Attorneys wanted him to sue for millions of dollars, but Rick never felt good about that. He was concerned that a lawsuit of that size would be too harmful to the responsible party. Also, the attorney told him that to pursue a case like that would require Rick to leave Bible college and stay home in Sandusky for court hearings and such. But Rick had surrendered his life completely to God for full-time vocational service and said that leaving college was a deal-breaker.

Finally, a settlement was awarded, and after legal fees and voluntarily giving two thirds of the amount to other burn victims, Rick was left with 20 percent of the original settlement of which he gave a significant portion to his local church. He didn't want his name affiliated with the gift in any way, so he quietly met with his pastor, who said it was the largest contribution the church had received in ten years.

Now well into retirement years, Rick is still serving Jesus. As founder and president of CHAMPS International, he leads mission trips to the Bahamas and other Caribbean Islands, not only to build churches and medical clinics, but to train young students so that they too can live generous lives for Christ. Rick is a living, breathing, willing example of what it means to truly *be* a generous person.

CHAPTER EIGHT

Freedom — It's all about contentment

Everything is wearisome beyond description. No matter how much we see, we are never satisfied. No matter how much we hear, we are not content.

ECCLESIASTES 1:8

Solomon was being brutally honest when he said that everything is wearisome, boring, unsatisfactory, because in our human condition we apparently don't know how to be content. It is true, dissatisfaction is unavoidable – especially if you are expecting the stuff of this world to fully satisfy.

The only antidote for this human condition and real path forward to a life of contentment is to find freedom through Jesus Christ. We were created in God's image, but our true identities were lost when original sin separated us from our loving Father, leaving a void that we try to fill with so many of the wrong things. But through Jesus Christ's blood atonement we have been reclaimed, redeemed, and returned to our true identities as children of God. And as His children, we are free from the bondage of sin's power over us. We are dead to sin (Rom. 6:11). We are alive – free – in Christ Jesus.

Because of our freedom from sin, we are no longer citizens of this world, but *citizens of heaven* (Phil. 3:20). Jesus promised His disciples, that He was preparing a place for His followers. He said, *I will come and get you, so that you will always be with me where I am* (John 14:3). The promise of our eternal destination is also mentioned in Hebrews 13:14, *This world is not our permanent home*, so as Christ followers we certainly shouldn't *feel* too much at home here. We shouldn't desire or be satisfied with material things which is why John urged us not to love the stuff here on earth (1 John 2:15). There is so much more waiting for us beyond this life, *a priceless inheritance—an inheritance that is kept in heaven for you, pure and undefiled, beyond the reach of change and decay* (1 Pet. 1:4).

Do you get it? We don't belong here. We are actually misfits in this world. Our focus should be on things above (Col. 3:2), not on the corruptible garbage all around us. Christian author Randy Alcorn said, "The more holdings we have on earth, the more likely we are to forget that we're citizens of another world..."[1] The stuff of this world holds us back from investing in our real purpose and our real home on the other side of this life. Stuff distracts us and holds us hostage demanding our attention, energy, and resources. Without knowing it we have become slaves to the master of materialism and love stuff above all else. Don't you think it's finally time to be free of it all?

FREEDOM IN CHRIST MAKES CONTENTMENT POSSIBLE

Years ago, coal miners used caged canaries to serve as an early detection for carbon monoxide and other toxic gases. When gases in the mine reached poisonous levels, the canaries would stop chirping and become agitated, signaling to the miners that it was time to exit the mine. (The birds were like pets, so the miners were faithful to take the cages out of the mine with them.) Until more modern technology was introduced, the "canary in the coal mine" served as the miners' only life-saving warning.

Figuratively speaking, for Christians, the bird that first signals the danger of materialism is clearly discontentment. The poisonous fumes of dissatisfaction will choke the breath of peace and joy out of your life. Always wanting more and never being satisfied is understandable for someone who has not received God's gift of grace but when a professing believer yearns for more and more of the world's goods, there is a real possibility that they have neglected their freedom in Jesus Christ. Sin sneaks up on us, so detecting discontentment early is an important key to breaking free from materialistic bondage.

Sixteenth century Puritan teacher Thomas Watson felt that contentment was a powerful tool to a victorious spiritual life, a noble conquest. He also believed that a gracious spirit, rather than a selfish one, was a contented spirit. He wrote, "The way for a man to be contented is not by raising his estate higher, but by bringing his heart lower."[2] A worldly "higher estate" is nothing compared to the humble surrender to Christ.

Your dissatisfaction either comes from a sinful, unregenerated heart, or one that is still clinging to worldly bondage. Paul was shocked when he learned that the Galatians were slipping back into sinful desires and told them, *You were running the race so well. Who has held you back from following the truth? It certainly isn't God, for he is the one who called you to freedom* (Gal. 5:7-8). Contentment in Christ enables you to resist worldly things because you understand that *the world offers only a craving for physical pleasure, a craving for everything we see, and pride in our achievements and possessions* (1 John 2:16).

LEARNING TO BE CONTENT

I have learned how to be content with whatever I have.

PHILIPPIANS 4:11

The simple definition of contentment is "a state of happiness and satisfaction." A contented soul is in a state of peace and rest, needing nothing. So, that means that a malcontent is in a rebellious state of dissatisfaction; they are restless, and on the prowl for something more. Contentment is based on an attitude of gratitude that we spoke about in chapter five. Contented people count their blessings and rejoice but even Paul admitted that he had to *learn* to be content.

But how does contentment connect to freedom? Let's review. Discontentment is an early warning sign that you are aimlessly looking for fulfillment in stuff instead of finding satisfaction in Jesus. Little by little you are relinquishing or surrendering your freedom and looking back to the world for satisfaction. So the question is, *Now that you know God (or should I say, now that God knows you), why do you want to go back again and become slaves once more to the weak and useless spiritual principles of this world?* (Gal. 4:9). So, when we are content, completely satisfied in Christ, and focused on things above, we are free – no longer encumbered with this world. Following are three simple lessons to help us learn contentment.

LESSON 1.
THERE IS A RIGHT WAY AND A WRONG WAY TO MEASURE WEALTH

Yet true godliness with contentment is itself great wealth.

1 TIMOTHY 6:6

In the material world, wealth is measured by the value of a person's total assets: how much is in the back account, the retirement fund, property investments, and so on. But as we've already discussed, these are all things that fade away. All things you will one day leave behind. So, in God's economy the currency is very different. His highest values are incorruptible.

Contentment becomes its own form of wealth because it removes the stress of debt and financial obligation from things you no longer need to immediately gratify yourself. The value of your relationship with God replaces the perishable commodities of this world, leaving you with a satisfied and grateful heart. Godly contentment also results from accepting Divine Ownership which is at the foundation of our full surrender to God. Apart from that, you are doomed to measure your wealth the wrong way. Only then will you see that the riches of abiding in Christ are a far greater value than all the stuff this world has to offer. Learning how to measure real wealth is an important lesson we all should learn.

LESSON 2.
CONTENTMENT KNOWS THE DIFFERENCE BETWEEN WANT AND NEED

And this same God who takes care of me will supply all your needs from his glorious riches, which have been given to us in Christ Jesus.

This verse in Philippians is a wonderful promise. Indeed, God will supply all our needs, but the verse can't be taken out of context, or it will set you up for a colossal disappointment. The Philippian church was a poor community, but they financially supported Paul because they believed in the cause and desired to see more believers added to the family of God. In the previous verses of this chapter, the apostle had already told them that he learned how to be content with very little, so it is unlikely that now Paul would be guaranteeing riches or perfect health in return for their support. This verse is not a quid pro quo promise and attempting to make this passage a blank check for anything we define as a need is a grave error.

First and foremost, Paul was assuring them that their *spiritual* needs would be met from God's *glorious riches which have been given to us in Christ Jesus.* God cares about our material needs, but this promise is a spiritual one based on the direct connection to the gift given to us through Jesus's debt payment of sin. But because Paul had been greatly moved by the immense sacrifice of the Philippians, it is clear that he implied a secondary element to this promise of meeting needs, but that depends greatly on knowing the difference between a want and a need. Understanding that difference is vital to living a spiritually contented life of freedom. So, we can embrace God's promise to provide abundant spiritual blessings and at the same time trust Him to meet our physical needs as well, being careful to merge actual accounts with scriptural truth. For instance, at the time Paul is writing to encourage this church, he himself is suffering in prison for his faith. Was God not supplying Paul's needs? Of course He was, and that is evidenced by Paul's letter. He is joyfully showing them that Christ supplies all those spiritual "intangible" needs regardless of circumstances.

Hebrews chapter 11 recalls stories of faith from people like Abraham, Jacob, and Moses, who with God's help *overthrew kingdoms, ruled with justice, and received what God had promised them. They shut the mouths of lions, quenched the flames of fire, and escaped death by the edge of the sword. Their weakness was turned to strength. They became strong in battle and put whole armies to flight* (verse 33-34). God supplied physical victory for each of these people. But the chapter also discloses the other side of the story saying, *But others were tortured, refusing to turn from God in order to be set free. They placed their hope in a better life after the resurrection* (verse 35).

So you see, the story doesn't always turn out the way we humanly *want* it to, but no matter the outcome, God supplied what these people of faith needed. In the latter cases, God provided the strength and courage necessary to even die for Him. In 2 Corinthians 4:17, Paul referred to this kind of suffering as small, assuring believers that it would not last long. Few of us would refer to torture or being chained in prison as a small thing but Paul could say this because he had a heavenly perspective. He understood that his life was dedicated to the eternal, not the temporal, and that through it all, God supplied every need. Peter adds to it by saying *after you have suffered a little while, he {God} will restore, support, and strengthen you, and he will place you on a firm foundation* (1 Pet. 5:10). In all these examples and in our lives still today, God supplies what we need, no matter what we endure. In troubling circumstances, God assured Paul, "*My grace is all you need. My power works best in weakness." So now I am glad to boast about my weaknesses, so that the power of Christ can work through me* (2 Cor. 12:9).

Nowhere in scripture or the history of the world, can you find a time when God was indebted to anyone. He has and will always supply our needs according to His riches in glory.

His grace and provision has been and always will be enough when you understand the difference between what you want on a human level and what you really need spiritually. Because everything in the tangible, material world will pass away, it must be viewed from an eternal perspective. If we can do that, the fuzzy lines between want and need become clear, even liberating. Otherwise, you are doomed to forever be a slave to stuff, imprisoned by greed and dissatisfaction.

Countless expenditures labeled "necessary," in reality often create hardships. But in spite of that, the debt train just keeps rolling down the tracks! According to the Federal Reserve Bank of New York, Americans continue racking up credit card debt at a record-setting pace. Credit card balances grew to 856 billion dollars in the fourth quarter of 2021, up 52 billion dollars (6.5%) from the previous quarter. That's the largest quarterly increase observed since the New York Fed began collecting this data 22 years ago.[3] Managing God's resources wisely means controlling debt, and that requires understanding the difference between want and need.

One of the greatest needs that we have is a place to live, but a recent article entitled *Americans Have Never Been So Much in Debt*, claims that mortgages, which are the largest component of household debt, have risen 230 billion dollars and now total over 10.67 trillion dollars.[4] For many people, the *want* of the bigger and better house has clouded their judgment, stretched them beyond their means and left them "house poor," creating the *need* to work longer hours just to make ends meet.

Another need is food, right? Well, according to an article featured in Forbes, Americans are eating out way too much. Sure, dining out has many benefits, including stress relief and social connections, but eating out too often can really put a dent in your wallet and cause you to live beyond your means. If you ever go over your limit or can't pay your bill on time, credit scores can be damaged, which in the long run also creates more financial stress.[5]

In addition to overspending at restaurants, Americans are eating their way to health problems such as diabetes and heart disease, which in turn leads to even greater financial burdens due to medications, doctor's visits, and lost wages from missing work. Overeating or eating out too often is an indulgence that repeatedly blurs the lines between want and need. Eating out may relieve some stress after a hard day of work but understand that over-indulging is just another road to self-gratification and one that can potentially mess with your family's finances.

We also need clothes to wear, but for some, shopping can become an addiction, causing individuals to spend money they don't have. One blogger put it this way, "Credit cards can be valuable financial tools if you use them correctly. But, on the flip side, if you don't understand a tool before you begin to introduce it into your routine, it might not always work in your favor. That was my relationship with credit cards for most of my 20s."[6] No one wants to be out of style and the desire to impress friends and even strangers can be a controlling motivator. When asked why she shopped to the point of racking up large debt, the response was, "Shopping and buying new clothing items felt like the one way to feel more confident in my own skin. Maybe I needed to spend to overcompensate for another emotional issue. Perhaps it's because society pushed me to that shallow of a level."[7]

Another real need, as most would agree, is preparing for the future, and while you may need the right education, what you *don't* need is crippling college debt. Discovering God's purpose for your life is a complicated and challenging endeavor. One thing is clear, Christian families should prayerfully consider the issue of devastating debt that comes with a degree from many colleges. In recent years the average cost of a four-year degree rose by 497 percent between the 1985-86 and 2017-18 academic years, more than twice the rate of inflation.[8] The cost has continued to skyrocket out of control leaving countless students buried in debt and in some cases, graduating with regret.

The follow up to this book, called *Not My Life*, could be immensely helpful for students and families when making financial decisions that will impact their future for decades to come. Most of all, determining what you need, not just what you want when it comes to education and preparation for the future, is the best way to make your decision and absolutely a critical element of contentment.

LESSON 3.
THERE IS A CONNECTION BETWEEN CONTENTMENT AND GRATITUDE

Let your roots grow down into him, and let your lives be built on him. Then your faith will grow strong in the truth you were taught, and you will overflow with thankfulness.

COLOSSIANS 2:7

This verse draws the connection between spiritual maturity and gratitude. People who are still slaves to stuff haven't grown deep relationship roots with God; they are shallow, making them easy prey to the world's seduction. That immaturity interferes with the ability to be thankful. Although we spoke briefly about gratitude in chapter five, it's important to go a little deeper into the subject here.

Gratefulness does not usually come easily or naturally, so it's imperative that we learn to be thankful, and that takes practice. Recently I passed out candy to almost two hundred different kids for Halloween, and because I was thinking about this idea of thankfulness, I took notes. Forty-seven kids said thank you when I put the candy in their bag. Of those children most had parents close by who had coached them what to say. To be fair, many of them were too young to even know what they were doing (which I suspect was to collect candy for their parents), so those very little ones get a pass, but it was interesting to me how few kids took the three seconds to simply say thank you. Still, this didn't surprise me too much because I happen to believe that true gratitude (and not just social politeness) is a learned behavior. I want to believe that the majority of parents are teaching this character quality to their children from the get-go, but I also fear that dissatisfied and ungrateful adults can also teach negative qualities to their kids without ever saying a word.

So how do we learn gratitude? Well, first and foremost, it needs to be **an intentional goal**. I think it's necessary to acknowledge your limitations. If you know that your habit for pessimism or ingratitude is conflicting with thankfulness, then purposefully strive to change it. Confess it to God and repent of it as often as you need every day. If you are unsure that you have that tendency, ask the Holy Spirit to reveal it to you. The warrior-poet King David prayed, *Search me, O God, and know my heart; test me and know my anxious thoughts. Point out anything in me that offends you and lead me along the path of everlasting life* (Psa. 139:23-24). The Holy Spirit will be faithful to shift your attitude and bring you to a place of thanksgiving.

Another way to learn gratitude is to **journal your blessings**. If you are looking in the right places, you can always find something praiseworthy to jot down. But remember that we are to give thanks in *all* circumstances, good or bad (1 Thess. 5:18). Finding the good in the bad is a little tougher assignment, but still it can be done. Someone with cancer may not feel thankful until they meditate on the fact that God will go with them through the painful circumstance. Even when we go through dark valleys, God is close beside us (Psa. 23:4). Journaling through the good times and even in the dark times will help you remember to be thankful in all circumstances.

Also **writing God's Word** is a good way to fill your mind with the positive things of God. The more you can engage your senses (in this case seeing and touching), the greater the learning experience will be. Many folks write gratitude scriptures on note cards and post them on mirrors, refrigerators, or any other place where they can be reminded throughout the day. Verses like Psalm 69:30, *Then I will praise God's name with singing, and I will honor him with thanksgiving.* Or Psalm 100:4, *Enter his gates with thanksgiving; go into his courts with praise. Give thanks to him and praise his name.* And one of my favorites, *Let everything that breathes sing praises to the Lord* (Psa. 150:6). One thing's for sure, there is an unlimited supply of precious thanksgiving reminders in God's Word.

Strangely enough, we can also become more thankful when we recall some of the negative situations of our past. Like most of you, Kathy and I have had some rough experiences in marriage, ministry, and even in managing God's resources but always when we reflect on those times, we can measure how far we've come together and how God's hand has always led us through to the other side. Many times, life's journey is along a broken road, but it is those situations that have drawn us closer to God. It is during those times that we have seen His love, grace, and mercy in action. So, if you can **be thankful for the rough patches in your past**, it means that those spiritual roots have grown.

While researching the whole concept of gratitude, I was reminded of an early Disney movie about the young girl Pollyanna, who played "the glad game." No matter what her circumstance, she found at least one way to be happy and thankful. Her positive attitude had a surprising effect on the whole community. In the same way, **gathering together with other believers** can also teach us to be grateful. The teaching of the Word and combining our audible praises to the Lord uplifts our spirits, giving us a sense of peace and contentment.

And finally, learning to be thankful comes from **habitual giving**. Generously caring for the needs of others instead of dwelling on ourselves, results in contentment as well as a thankfulness that we had the ability to help someone else. Then we find ourselves looking for more opportunities to help others. Giving also means bringing *an offering and coming before Him* to *worship the Lord in the beauty of holiness!* (1 Chron. 16:29). Whether through an offering or volunteering your talents or both, it's all part of the giving experience and helpful in growing a thankful heart.

Ingratitude steals your potential to be rich in contentment, and the lack of contentment affects your freedom from the things of this world. I encourage you to spend some time thoughtfully comparing the eternal against the things that perish. Perhaps the following examples will be helpful.

- I can be content without paying five dollars for a bottled water at Starbucks… but I can't live without Jesus, the living water in my life (John 7:38).

- I can be content without Nike's newest shoes that promise to make me run fast…but I can't run the race of life without Jesus (Heb. 12:1).

- I can be content without excessive costly restaurant and take-out delivery… but I can't live without Jesus, the bread of life that feeds my soul (John 6:35).

- I can be content without the approval of people… but I can't live without God's favor and approval (Gal. 1:10).

I pray you will begin to clearly see the things that matter the most. Letting go of all the world's stuff and embracing God's Divine Ownership is the ultimate path to contentment and freedom.

CHOOSE FREEDOM TODAY AND EVERY DAY

We receive God's promise of freedom only by believing in Jesus Christ.

GALATIANS 3:22

Then choose today whom you will serve…but as for me and
my family, we will serve the Lord.

Even after you've found freedom through the blood atonement of Jesus, there will still be times when the gods of materialism try to draw you back. The Prodigal could tell you firsthand that it makes no sense to trade a relationship of love and freedom with the Father for the temporary pleasures stuff might bring. Mary Magdalene would likewise urge you to follow Christ instead of offering yourself to the world. Joshua would say choose moving forward with God over turning back. I pray you will make the right choice to follow the Savior and become a faithful steward who contentedly lives free from the stuff of this world. It should be an easy choice, because if you have the faith to trust Jesus to redeem you from sin, then you also have the faith to trust Him for all your needs. Above all, remember that the journey of a faithful steward leads to true freedom.

Let us strip off every weight that slows us down, especially the
sin that so easily trips us up. And let us run with endurance
the race God has set before us.

HEBREWS 12:1

217

WHAT DOES FREEDOM FROM STUFF LOOK LIKE?

Freedom from materialism allows you to do what God leads you to do, because you are no longer holding back, reaching for the things that don't last. That was the story for Greg and Lisa who felt God leading them to fly halfway around the globe to change the life on one precious baby girl, and in the end change their lives as well.

Already blessed with four beautiful and perfectly healthy children, their cup was full and running over. Working a steady job to provide for their active family, Greg was content with four children; but there was a stirring in Lisa's soul for at least one more. She had always dreamed of a large family, and even started a licensed in-home daycare because she loved having more babies and toddlers around. So, she began to pray for Greg to change his mind and to be open to having more children.

Her answered prayer began to manifest when Greg went on an extended mission's trip to Jamaica. God planted a small seed in his heart, and shortly after that, Greg began to hear about the needs of children born into sickness and poverty in Ethiopia. As part of his research into the matter, Greg attended a presentation in Cleveland, Ohio, and was directed to the HOPE agency that helps Americans adopt needy children.

The process was at first very discouraging. None of the children presented to them through pictures and personal information seemed to be the right fit for the family. Oddly enough, Lisa had always wanted a little girl that she could name "Joy." Then one day a precious baby girl's image came across their computer screen. Her name was Serkalem, which means "happiness at all times." Greg and Lisa knew this was the one – the little child who was an answer to prayer and the one to complete their family.

But it would cost them.

In fact, the agency had to put Serkalem's adoption on hold until certain deposits were collected, deposits that they just didn't have yet. There was still a need for several thousands of dollars more, and while some friends advised them not to pursue the adoption any longer, the couple was more determined than ever to follow through. Greg understood their concerns, but at the same time said, "We don't all have the same flame." He knew that their passion for this little child was God-given, and because He is such an amazing God, at just the right time a miraculous donation was given to their family for the exact amount needed to insure that Serkalem would soon be theirs.

Finally, on January 7, 2010, Greg and Lisa traveled to Ethiopia and for the first time held their new baby girl in their arms. As it turns out, January 7 is the day Ethiopian Orthodox Christians celebrate Christmas, and what a celebration this was! Today, Lilibet Joy, (middle name Serkalem), as she is now known is an active, healthy, beautiful girl who loves skateboarding and all kinds of sports. She is an extraordinary person who in all likelihood would never have survived were it not for Greg and Lisa's freedom to follow God.

Greg and Lisa's story is an example of total freedom for many reasons. They had reached that mile marker close to being empty nesters. Maybe at this time in life, they could travel together, or do some updating of the house, or get a newer vehicle, but when God brought them face to face with an opportunity to test their faith and change their lives, they chose to set aside the familiar and comfortable, and to not be controlled by the currents of the world. They were free to listen to God's voice in their hearts instead.

As long as I've known this couple I can say without doubt that they believe in Divine Ownership. They do not chase after material things, and have always trusted God to provide their needs, all the while faithfully giving back to God their time, abilities, and finances. They are "freedom stewards," and even now continue to embrace all that God still has planned for their family.

Perspective — It's all clear now

Here now is my final conclusion: Fear God and obey his commands, for this is everyone's duty. God will judge us for everything we do, including every secret thing, whether good or bad.

ECCLESIASTES 12:13-14

As we wrap up this study, I think I'd like to start with a story:

Jesus said, "There was a certain rich man who was splendidly clothed in purple and fine linen and who lived each day in luxury. At his gate lay a poor man named Lazarus who was covered with sores. Finally, the poor man died and was carried by the angels to sit beside Abraham at the heavenly banquet. The rich man also died and was buried, and he went to the place of the dead. There, in torment, he saw Abraham in the far distance with Lazarus at his side. "The rich man shouted, 'Father Abraham, have some pity!

Send Lazarus over here to dip the tip of his finger in water and cool my tongue. I am in anguish in these flames.' "*But Abraham said to him, 'Son, remember that during your lifetime you had everything you wanted, and Lazarus had nothing. So now he is here being comforted, and you are in anguish*" (Luke 16:19-25).

For the rich man, it was just too late.

I have a lot of contemporary stories like that of the rich man. Individuals on their death bed who look back with regret, lamenting the way they lived. Many confessing a wasted life saying they wish they'd done things differently. Too selfish. Didn't do enough. Too focused on all the wrong things. As a pastor for nearly four decades, I have made more hospital visits and done more funerals than I even care to count. Regret has not been uncommon for many of the conversations that took place during those final sobering moments. It is sad that anyone would wait till they are about to meet their Maker to suddenly wise up.

But there is a flip side to those stories, and these are the ones I want to tell you about. These are the ones who arrived at the finish line of this earthly pilgrimage with rejoicing, and they all have one thing in common: They had made the right choice regarding stuff. They ran the race and finished strong, and they did it by keeping their eyes on Jesus (Hebrews 12:2) and not on the world.

Some were rich, many were poor, and they came from every background imaginable, but they all possessed a peace in those final moments that you could practically feel. Almost touchable, tangible. Somewhere in their life's journeys they had learned the truth about stuff and made the right choice to surrender their lives to be God's stewards. They did not fear the day of judgment referred to in the passage from Ecclesiastes but possessed a rare and genuine sense of awe that humbly moved them to obey the truth that everything had always belonged to God.

One Christian mother told me that the tithe she gave every month was hard, but that God had blessed more than she could imagine. She said, "Today my kids are my friends and I leave this world knowing they all love Jesus." Another elderly gentleman who had come from the impoverished mountains of West Virginia told how he and his wife had chosen to build a simple house with no debt, paying and building just a little bit each year, so that they could also financially give back to God for eternal purposes. Then there was the couple who started their faith journey late in life. They told me how they were previously buried in debt as a result of their own doing, but that the last years of their life were the best because that's when they learned to put God first in their giving, both financially and as faithful volunteers in the church.

I also recall being at the bedside of an elderly saint named Herb. He was always a lover of God who faithfully taught a Sunday School class each week. Such a blessing he was to me. When his time came, the family called me in to pray. There he was, surrounded by all his precious loved ones. He motioned for me to come closer, and he whispered in my ear, "Today is the best day of my life." Herb had lived a beautiful life, no regrets, no worry, only complete peace, contentment, and freedom.

I have heard so many precious affirmations just like Herb's from givers and never once did any of them say they regretted their lives of generosity. Not a single one of them said they wished they had bought more stuff. Their vantage point was an end of life assessment, and they all rejoiced knowing they had lived their lives in the light of God's truth. They died in peace and awoke to the Heavenly Father's affirming words, "*well done my good and faithful servant*" (Matt. 25:21). And in that moment, they realized the race for the eternal over the temporal had been won.

After reading this book, some will easily embrace the scriptural truths outlined in this study and immediately put the principles of Divine Ownership into practice. Others will begin the journey and perhaps a few months later begin to question the sustainability of a life of faith. This is a common fear, and these folks will need to resolve that fear by refreshing their hearts with the scriptural process outlined in this book that originally inspired them to begin the journey.

And still others will push back against the conviction deep in their hearts that this is the right thing to do. The spiritual conflict will be a struggle like treading the waters of financially storm-tossed seas until they reach out for the rescuing hand of Jesus. He will never force anyone to take His hand, but He will allow the storms to continue for anyone who rejects His rescue plan. I've known many people who have spent most of their lives treading financial waters. Most of the time their lives are full of discord and dissatisfaction. What can I say, some people are slow learners.

Psalm 37:4 says, *Take delight in the Lord, and he will give you the desires of your heart.* Some mistakenly think this verse means you can expect God to give you anything you want or ask for, but in reality the passage is saying so much more. It's talking about the change of heart we experience when we surrender to Christ. The desire for things we once thought we wanted, have changed. Like Paul when he said, *I consider everything a loss because of the surpassing worth of knowing Christ*

Jesus my Lord, for whose sake I have lost all things. I consider them garbage, that I may gain Christ (Phil. 3:8).

My missionary friend Greg Lyons would whole-heartedly agree with Paul's summation. Not only is Greg a seminary president, but he is also the founder of Global Surge, an organization that takes the Gospel throughout Asia. In his and his family's nearly 30 years of dedicated service world-wide, they have so far seen over one million lost souls come to know Jesus as their Savior.[1] Greg could have chosen to use his business savvy and leadership skills to become a wealthy man here in the U.S., but Greg wouldn't change a thing, because he measures his wealth differently.

The truth is you may never fully see the return on your eternal investments until you stand before God one day in heaven. It's then that you will meet the people whose lives were forever changed because you gave an offering or because you donated your time and abilities to a life-saving ministry project. But for now, you can look with your eyes of faith to see the results to come.

God has a plan for His people and His church. Nothing asked of us in scripture is unattainable. For every command or mission, the Church has been given, there is a solution built into the life we Christians have been called to lead. The Great Commission found in Matthew 28, is completely possible if the Church chooses the life of faithfully stewarding everything in their care. God never asks us to do anything that He has not already made a provision for. We just need to be willing to follow His plan for our lives. His purpose becomes reality when we practice His principles. Only then will the mission of the Church be fully funded and empowered because you have become free from the controlling power of stuff.

Our view through the light of God's truth allows us to see the goodness of God and connects us directly to an understanding of the ownership question. When we see that God is a loving Father who supplies what we need, when we need it, we are then capable of being content with what we have. We can live our lives with a deep assurance that God has taken notice and that rich or poor, He wants to use us in His plans. But in order to do that, we must surrender it all to Him. Then when our time has come to measure our earthly lives, our hearts can be filled with a gratitude that rejoices in His goodness and honestly says, "It was never my stuff."

"I have held many things in my hands, and I have lost them all; but whatever I have placed in God's hands, that I still possess."

MARTIN LUTHER

Stuff to Think
and Talk About

CHAPTER ONE:
STUFF – IT CAN'T MAKE YOU HAPPY

1. How would you describe the way you feel when you are tempted to obtain something you don't have but know it may not be in your best interest? For insights into how temptation plays out in your life, refer to the account of how Adam and Eve were tempted. (Genesis 3; 1 Corinthians 10:13)

2. Can you remember a time when you obtained something that you really wanted, but later you were disappointed by the stuff you thought you had to have? Write down what the stuff was that did not bring you lasting happiness to remind you about how stuff has a limited shelf-life. (Job 15:29; Luke 12:16-21; James 1:10)

3. If stuff can't make you happy, what do you believe is the source of lasting happiness? (Ecclesiastes 5:10; Psalm 41:1; Psalm 89:15; Luke 6:22-23)

4. What are some of the things you need to do, or not do in order to experience a truly meaningful life? Make a list of the things you can incorporate into your life that will last. (Psalms 1; Proverbs 17:17; 1 Corinthians 13:13)

5. What is the difference between happiness and long term contentment? (Luke 6:24; Philippians 4:11; 1 Timothy 6:6)

CHAPTER TWO:
OWNERSHIP – IT'S ALL GOD'S STUFF

1. Who really owns all the stuff and why is it important to understand this truth? (1 Chronicles 29:11)

2. What does the story in Matthew 24 teach us about the different ways people manage the resources they have under their control? (Matthew 24:45-47)

3. Why do those who possess much of the world's goods have such a difficult time accepting the idea that everything belongs to God? (Matthew 19:16-30)

4. What can we learn from Jesus on selflessness and the value of stuff? How would you describe your own approach for handling stuff? (Mark 8:35)

5. In your own words describe what Divine Ownership means to you. How do you practice this spiritual truth? (James 1:22)

CHAPTER THREE:
RELATIONSHIP – IT COMES WITH PRIVILEGES

1. What is the basis for the privileges we enjoy as followers of Jesus Christ? (Romans 5:2)

2. How much does God love and value you? What are some of the blessings you inherited from God when you were born again into His family? (Matthew 6:26)

3. What are some of the ways that suffering for Jesus opens privileged opportunities? (Philippians 1:29; 1 Peter 4:16)

4. How has the privilege of prayer strengthened your relationship with God? (Hebrews 4:16; Philippians 4:6)

5. What are some ways you can take advantage of the privilege of telling others about Jesus? (Romans 1:5)

CHAPTER FOUR:
TRUST – IT MUST BE GROWN

1. What is an example of a promise God has made that you have embraced and then trusted Him to keep? (Hebrews 10:23)

2. What are some ways God guides you in your life if you are trusting Him? (Psalm 18:30; Psalm 143:8; 1 Timothy 6:17-20)

3. What is something you have trusted God for to help you overcome? (Galatians 2:20)

4. How does trusting God help you overcome fears and make you feel safe? (Proverbs 29:25; John 17:15; 2 Timothy 4:18)

5. Can you describe a time in your life when you took a first step toward trusting Jesus but then took your eyes off of Him and replaced the trust with doubt? (Matthew 14:27-50)

CHAPTER FIVE:
PEACE – IT'S A REAL THING

1. What should we focus on in order to experience what the Bible calls *perfect peace?* (Isaiah 26:3)

2. What is the source of real peace and what are some of the benefits for those who are experiencing peace? (John 14:27)

3. How does the way you treat others affect the potential you have for living a life of peace? (1 Peter 3:9-11)

4. What are some lessons that can be learned from the story of the Prodigal Son relating to the world's ability to bring lasting peace, friends, and family? (Luke 15)

5. How important is contentment when it comes to peace of mind and your ability to be a giver? (Philippians 4:11-12)

CHAPTER SIX:
USEFULNESS – IT'S FOR EVERYONE

1. How does your spiritual growth impact your ability to live a useful life? (2 Peter 1:8; 1 Corinthians 13:11)

2. From the *Seven Bible heroes you've never heard of* section of Chapter 6, which one of these individuals can you most identify with and why?

3. In a world of celebrity personalities and influencers that become models to follow and imitate, who are we as believers to pattern our life after? (Ephesians 5:1-2)

4. Why is everyone in the body of the Church important? (I Corinthians 12:14-18; Romans 12:4-5)

5. What is the most important gift you can give and how is this gift useful? (2 Corinthians 8:5)

CHAPTER SEVEN:
GENEROSITY – IT'S WHO YOU ARE

1. Look up the following verses about generosity and reflect on how they might be applied to your life today. (Isaiah 32:8; Acts 2:46; Philemon 1:6)

2. How does our generosity in this world impact eternity? (1 Timothy 6:17-19; Matthew 6:19-21)

3. What is the best heart attitude for a person of generosity? (2 Corinthians 9:7)

4. Are those with limited resources exempt from being generous? (2 Corinthians 8:1-3)

5. What is the connection between generosity and the law of sowing and reaping? (2 Corinthians 9:6)

CHAPTER EIGHT:
FREEDOM – IT'S ALL ABOUT CONTENTMENT

1. Why are those enslaved by stuff never free and never satisfied? (Ecclesiastes 1:8)

2. What has made it possible for you to be free to give? (John 8:32; Romans 6:18; 2 Corinthians 8:3)

3. How is the way the world measures wealth different from the way God measures it? (1 Timothy 6:6)

4. How do you define the difference between a want and a need? (Philippians 4:19)

5. What are some ways that being thankful results in your being more content? (Colossians 2:7; 1 Thessalonians 5:18; Psalm 69:30; Psalm 100:4)

NOTES

INTRODUCTION:
STUFF – IT'S ALL AROUND US

1. Alexander Harris, "U.S. Storage Industry Statistics," Jan 27, 2021, https://www.sparefoot.com/self-storage/news/1432-self-storage-industry-statistics/

CHAPTER 1:
STUFF – IT CAN'T MAKE YOU HAPPY

1. Michael Bond, "The Psychological Power of Possessions," March 24, 2014, www.newscientist.com/article/mg22129620-900-stuff-the-psychological-power-of-possessions/

2. Ibid.

3. Henry Ward Beecher, *Freedom and War* (Boston: Ticknor and Fields, 1863).

4. Neel Burton, "Is Greed Good?," Psychology Today, October 6, 2014, www.psychologytoday.com/us/blog/hide-and-seek/201410/is-greed-good

5. Marty Steinberg and Scot Cohn, "Bernie Madoff, Mastermind of the Nation's Biggest Investment Fraud, Dies at 82," CNBC, April 14, 2019, https://www.cnbc.com/2021/04/14/bernie-madoff-dies-mastermind-of-the-nations-biggest-investment-fraud-was-82.html

6. Evan Anderson, "Super Bowl LVI Commercials Take Lighter Approach," February 13, 2022, https://www.nbcdfw.com/news/local/super-bowl-lvi-commercials-take-lighter-approach/2888301/

7. A. Guttman, "Advertising Spending in North America," Statista, July 1, 2022, https://www.statista.com/statistics/429036/advertising-expenditure-in-north-america/

8. Mother Teresa, *No Greater Love,* (Novato: New World Library, 2001).

CHAPTER 2:
OWNERSHIP – IT'S ALL GOD'S STUFF

1. David Fisher, "Patek Philippe-Good Advertising or Bad Advertising?," Highsnobiety, 2018, https://www.highsnobiety.com/p/patek-philippe-good-advertising-or-bad-advertising/

2. Alan Mozes, "Givers Really Are Happier Than Takers," WebMD, August 2017, https://www.webmd.com/balance/news/20170815/givers-really-are-happier-than-takers

3. Ibid.

4. Lyle Daly, "The 8 Biggest Benefits of Being Generous," The Ascent, a Motley Fool Service, July 17, 2021, https://www.webmd.com/balance/news/20170815/givers-really-are-happier-than-takers

5. Barbara Rainey, "What's Hiding in My Heart," Enter Thine Home, January 4, 2017, https://everthinehome.com/whats-hiding-heart/

6. John Newton and William Cowper, *The Onley Hymns,* (Curiosmith, 2011, original publication 1779).

7. Joshua Bontrager, blogger and publisher, "Intentional or Accidental Christians? Lessons from the Life of C.T. Studd," January 2018, https://joshuabontrager.com/lessons-from-the-life-of-c-t-studd/

8. "41 Church Giving Statistics You Should know" Vanco Faith, https://www.vancopayments.com/egiving/church-giving-statistics-tithing

CHAPTER 3:
RELATIONSHIP – IT COMES WITH PRIVILEGES

1. "Hurricane Andrew: Remembering the Devastation 30 Years Later," Channel 6 South Florida NBC, August 2022, https://www.nbcmiami.com/news/local/hurricane-andrew-remembering-the-devastation-30-years-later/2836964/

2. Sheryl Nance-Nash, "Is the Bible the Ultimate Financial Guide?" May 2012, Forbes,

https://www.forbes.com/sites/sherylnancenash/2012/05/24/is-the-bible-the-ultimate-financial-guide/?sh=4e413cac6493

3. Ibid.

CHAPTER 4:
TRUST – IT MUST BE GROWN

1. Corrie Ten Boom, *The Hiding Place*, (New York: Bantam Books, 1971).

2. "What's Preventing You from Trusting God?" Thomas Nelson, October 2018, www.thomasnelsonbibles.com/blog/whats-preventing-you-trusting-god/

3. Dan Babkoff, "IBM Refused to Lay Off Workers for Decades, and Then America Had to Rethink Its Entire Corporate Strategy," June 2016, https://www.businessinsider.com/ibm-corporate-america-history-2016-6

4. "Five Jobs That Will Not Return Even After COVID 19 is Over: Top Five Trends from the World of Work," Adecco Group, September 2020, https://www.adeccogroup.com/future-of-work/latest-insights/five-jobs-that-will-not-return-even-after-covid-19-is-over-top-5-trends-from-the-world-of-work/

5. Helen Howarth Lemmel, composer, "Turn your eyes upon Jesus," from *Gospel Truth in Song*, (Harry Clark Publications, 1924).

6. E.M. Bounds, *The Complete Works of E.M. Bounds on Prayer,* (Grand Rapids: Baker Books, 2004).

7. Dick Eastman, *The Hour that Changes the World,* (Grand Rapids: Baker Book House, 1978).

8. Max Lucado, *Just Like Jesus*, (Nashville: Word Publishing, 1998).

CHAPTER 5:
PEACE – IT'S THE REAL THING

1. Josiah Bates, "U.S. Crime is Still Dramatically Higher Than Before the Pandemic," Time, July 28, 2022, https://time.com/6201797/crime-murder-rate-us-high-2022/

2. Laura Smith, PhD., and Charles Elliott, PhD., *Depression for Dummies* (Hoboken: John Wiley & Sons, 2021).

3. Ibid.

4. Rick Warren, *The Purpose Driven Life,* (Grand Rapids: Zondervan, 2002).

5. Watchman Nee, *Quoteslyfe.com*, December 2, 2022 https://www.quoteslyfe.com/quote/An-unpeaceful-mind-cannot-operate-normally-1147122

6. Max Lucado, *Just Like Jesus*, (Nashville: Word Publishing, 1998).

7. God-shaped hole is a concept dating back to the 17th century theologian, Elaise Pascal, which has found its way into contemporary music.

8. Max Lucado, *Traveling Light,* (Nashville: Word Publishing, 2001).

CHAPTER 6:
USEFULNESS – IT'S FOR EVERYONE

1. David McCullough, *Pioneers,* (New York: Simon & Schuster, 2019).

2. Ibid.

3. Richard Beeman, *Our lives, Our fortunes and our Sacred Honor, the Forging of American Independence, 1774-1776,* (New York: Basic Books, 2013).

4. Benjamin Franklin, "From Benjamin Franklin to Abiah Franklin, 12 April 1750," National Archives Founders Online, American Philosophical Society and Yale University, Founders.archives.gov/documents/Franklin/01-02-02,

5. Thurston Clark, *Ask Not, the Inauguration of John F. Kennedy and the Speech that Changed America,* (New York: Henry Holt and Company, 2004).

CHAPTER 7:
GENEROSITY – IT'S WHO YOU ARE

1. Francis Chan, *Crazy Love*, (Colorado Springs: David C. Cook, 2013).

2. Jennifer Taylor, "The Widow's Mite," Samford University, Special Collection Treasures, July 2005, https://library.samford.edu/special/treasures/2005/mite.html

3. Dominick Reuter, "Billionaires Richer and Stingier Than Ever, Insider, October 10, 2021, https://www.businessinsider.com/billionaires-richer-and-stingier-than-ever-forbes-400-list-2021-10

4. Raj Raghunathan, "Why Rich People Aren't as Happy as They Could Be," Harvard Business Review, June 8, 2016, https://hbr.org/2016/06/why-rich-people-arent-as-happy-as-they-could-be

5. Max Lucado, *Just Like Jesus*, (Nashville: Word Publishing, 1998).

6. Stephen Furtick, *Crash the Chatterbox*, (Colorado Springs: Multnomah Books,2014).

7. Steven Zauderer, "Key Average Attention Span Statistics," crossrivertherapy.com, November 15, 2022, https://www.crossrivertherapy.com/average-human-attention-span

8. Tony Robbins, *Unlimited Power*, (New York: Free Press, a division of Simon & Schuster, 1986).

9. Eckert Tolle, *The Power of Now*, (Novato: New World Library, 1999).

10. Gary Zukav, *The Seat of the Soul*, (NY, Simon & Schuster, 1989).

11. Thomas Keneally, *Schindler's List*, (New York: Simon and Schuster, 1982). Movie: *Schindler's List*, Steven Spielberg, Director, DreamWorks, Feb 1994.

12. Rick Schuessler, *Tested by Fire*, (Shelbyville: Bible and Literature Missionary Foundation)

CHAPTER 8:
FREEDOM – IT'S ALL ABOUT CONTENTMENT

1. Randy Alcorn, "Having a Pilgrim Mentality About Money and Possessions," Eternal Perspective Ministries, 11 April 2016, https://www.epm.org/blog/2016/Apr/11/pilgrim-mentality

2. Thomas Watson, *The Art of Divine Contentment: An Exposition of Philippians 4:11*, (In Modern English, all rights reserved Jason Roth, reprinted 2017).

3. Erica Giovanetti, "Credit Card Debt is Surging at a Record-High Rate, NY Fed Reports," Foxbusiness, February 18, 2022, https://www.foxbusiness.com/personal-finance/credit-card-debt-balances-grow-record-rate

4. Anneken Tappe, "Americans Have Never Been in So Much Debt," CNN Business, November 11, 2021, https://www.cnn.com/2021/11/09/economy/fed-household-debt-inflation/index.html

5. Lillian Guevara-Castro, "Why Eating Out is Destroying Your Credit," Bad Credit, updated June 23, 2020, https://www.badcredit.org/why-eating-out-is-ruining-your-credit/ updated June 23, 2020, https://www.badcredit.org/why-eating-out-is-ruining-your-credit/

6. Alyssa Davis, "My Clothing Addiction Was Killing My Credit," mixedupmoney.com, January 12, 2021, https://mixedupmoney.com/clothing-addiction-killing-credit/

7. Ibid.

8. Erik Sherman, "College Tuition is Rising at Twice the Inflation Rate While Students Learn at Home," Forbes, August 31, 2020, https://www.forbes.com/sites/zengernews/2020/08/31/college-tuition-is-rising-at-twice-the-inflation-rate-while-students-learn-at-home/?sh=2c62f6ba2f98

CONCLUSION:
PERSPECTIVE – IT'S ALL BEHIND US

1. Greg Lyons of Global Surge: globalsurge.org